Critical Affect

Critical Affect
The Politics of Method

Ashley Barnwell

EDINBURGH
University Press

Edinburgh University Press is one of the leading university presses in the UK. We publish academic books and journals in our selected subject areas across the humanities and social sciences, combining cutting-edge scholarship with high editorial and production values to produce academic works of lasting importance. For more information visit our website: edinburghuniversitypress.com

Edinburgh University Press Ltd
The Tun – Holyrood Road, 12(2f) Jackson's Entry, Edinburgh EH8 8PJ

First published in hardback by Edinburgh University Press 2020

Typeset in 10.5/13 Bembo by
IDSUK (DataConnection) Ltd

A CIP record for this book is available from the British Library

ISBN 978 1 4744 5132 1 (hardback)
ISBN 978 1 4744 5133 8 (paperback)
ISBN 978 1 4744 5135 2 (webready PDF)
ISBN 978 1 4744 5134 5 (epub)

Contents

Acknowledgements

During the process of writing this book I have been supported and encouraged by mentors, colleagues and friends. First and foremost, Vicki Kirby has been an invaluable mentor to me. It is difficult to convey the extent of my gratitude to her – she has inspired me to be curious, to be loyal to my questions, to take intellectual work seriously and to write a decent sentence. The unwavering acuity, richness and honesty of her guidance made this project possible. I am also grateful to academics at UNSW where I began this project as a PhD student, including Melanie White, Helen Pringle and Ursula Rao. Andrew Metcalfe, a generous mentor and friend, has pushed me in good ways and shown me faith. The *Mull* reading group has been a rich space for nutting out ideas; I thank especially the 7th Day Afternoonists – Florence Chiew, Will Johncock and Jac Dalziell – for five years of whatsapp smarts and jokes. Fellow denizens of 'the Lab' kept me afloat with their friendship – extra thanks to Rosemary Grey, Beck Pearse, Emilie Auton, Scott McBride, Lorraine Burdett, and Patricia Morgan. With a strange magic, Kate Bush's wintery album *50 Words for Snow* created a sonic haven in which to write; I listened to it over and over, no doubt its rhythms turn up in the text.

I am grateful to my colleagues @unimelbsoc, especially my partner-in-schemes Signe Ravn for her daily support and comradery. Special thanks to Geoff Mead for reading chapters of this book as I revised them, offering erudite and kind comments and politely correcting my French. The School of Social and Political Sciences at the University of Melbourne provided valuable research leave which allowed me time to think and write. My thanks to

Amy Vanderharst for her research assistance, and her inside scoop on the latest conspiracy theories. In fruitful conversations, Jennifer Mason, Chris Healy and Daniel McCarthy have also helped me think about the parameters and aims of this project. I thank Mary Holmes for her intellect and humour and for hosting me at the University of Edinburgh in early 2019, affording me much needed time to immerse myself in the manuscript. Walking past the architectural mash-up of the Quarter Mile every day affirmed for me how the old and the new can work together. Many thanks to Carol Macdonald and Kirsty Woods at EUP for their professionalism and support, and to EUP's anonymous reviewers for valuable feedback. Finally, my greatest debt is to my mother, Maree, and my family for their support and pride in my efforts, and to Joe for his care, patience and love.

A version of Chapter 3 is published as 'Entanglements of evidence in the turn against critique', in *Cultural Studies*, 2015, 30: 6, 906–25, and republished with permission of Taylor & Francis. Chapter 5 appears as 'Creative paranoia: Affect and social method', in *Emotion, Space & Society*, 2016, 20, 10–17, reprinted with permission from Elsevier. A few sections from Chapter 1 appear in 'Enduring divisions: Questions of method and value in the sociology of literature', in *Cultural Sociology*, 2015, 9: 4, 550–66, and are reprinted with permission from Sage.

Introduction

Following the rising interest in affective aspects of social experience, there has been a rush to set aside poststructural critique and embrace methods that are seen to be more in touch with emotional truths and embodied sensations. The central claim is that critique has become routinely suspicious, always searching for hidden motives or seeking to debunk false consciousness, and is therefore unable to read people's everyday beliefs for 'what they are'. Bruno Latour (2004), for example, argues that critique has now 'run out of steam' and likens the critic to a conspiracy theorist, obsessed with unveiling hidden motives. Eve Kosofsky Sedgwick (1997) similarly writes that critics are stuck in a cycle of 'paranoid reading' and need to adopt more 'reparative' approaches to read cultural texts. Inspired by these influential arguments, a variety of methods associated with affect, non-representational and actor-network theories have been promoted as the way forward (Law 2004; Thrift 2007; Liljeström and Paasonen 2010; Felski 2015). Though this is framed as a new turn in theory and method, *Critical Affect* argues that the perceived split between poststructural critique and affect theory reiterates an enduring, interdisciplinary debate about which genre best captures the emotional complexity of social life, a debate that remains provocative and unresolved.

Scientists, sociologists, novelists, auto/biographers and journalists have all grappled with the question of whether the verifiability of fact or the emotional truth of fiction can most accurately capture the dynamic and intricate nature of social experience. From the 'two cultures' debate between scientists and literary scholars in the 1950s to more recent conflicts between social theorists and scientists in the 1990s 'science wars', the fraught question of which method produces the most authentic account has been at the forefront of intellectual debate. However, in most cases, efforts to answer this question have been stymied by the need to privilege fact over fiction or vice versa. The recent turn from critical to affective concerns in cultural theory similarly presents the problem of method as a choice. Scholars are often asked to choose structure or affect, critique or creativity, detection or description. But should our notion of methods be so fixed and divided? Indeed, might social life be more complex than a straightforwardly critical *or* affective approach alone can truly capture?

Via close readings of pivotal method proposals in the 'critique of critique', I draw attention to the overlooked methodological implications of this popular turn in theory and unsettle the claim that critique – as a method geared towards evidence and revelation – cannot engage with the mutable dynamics of affect. Rather than promoting judgement over intuition, or epistemology over ontology, this book rethinks the means by which we differentiate them. It shows that seemingly agonistic categories are full of crossover and complexity by drawing out the creative and sensitive aspects of critique and the censoring and coercive capacities of affect. By putting theory in dialogue with popular culture, I argue that suspicions about how we determine and represent truth still drive the turn to affect and ontology and resonate with immediate cultural concerns about transparency, conspiracy and contingent truths. In this context, critical attention can be seen as an affective and contemporary response rather than an outdated method. Wary and hopeful at the same time, it is a vital social method for people trying to survive in political climates where structures and the measures by which they are valued and verified threaten to shift at any moment.

This book therefore offers a clear intervention into affect theory, but also opens up new areas of interest and inquiry for the field. It takes the turn to affect as a point of entry into wider ethical queries about how we circumscribe and verify arguments. Focusing on overlooked issues of method, it parses out underlying questions about how we determine what will and will not qualify as a proper genre, an authentic identity or an affective impulse as well as how these decisions limit the kinds of questions we can ask and answer. Overall, I argue for a less divisive approach to the way scholars define methods and fix their values. I ask not whether we should choose either affect *or* critique, felt *or* factual truths, emotion *or* evidence, but rather what is at stake in making such selections.

Importantly, however, while *Critical Affect* intervenes in existing discussions about how to most authentically represent social life, it steers away from choosing which method is finally and exclusively the most veracious. Rather, it meditates upon how and why we make such decisions, and what these appraisals tell us about how we value and use truth, facts and evidence. The book explores why we invest certain ways of explaining something with more authority or worth than others, and if our commitment to certain modes of representation limits the scope of what can be recognised or revealed. It is interested in how our subscription to certain genres, to set identities with recognisable characteristics, creates important forms of social cohesion but also terms of exclusivity. Or, put simply, how do our questions shape our answers, and vice versa?

Locating the Politics of Method in the Ontological Turn

To set the scene, in recent years we have witnessed 'an ontological turn' toward post-human theories across the social sciences and humanities. These interventions decentre politics from human agency, question the primacy of rational forces and attend to the material – be it bodies, animals, objects, machines or environments. Such theories include speculative realism (Meillassoux 2008), object oriented ontology (Harman 2018), new materialism (Barad 2007; Dolphijn and van der Tuin 2012), affect theory (Massumi 1995; Sedgwick and Frank 1995), actor-network theory (Latour 2005; Law and Hassard 1999), and feminist science studies (Stengers 2015; Haraway 2007). These schools are diverse but share a structure in common, that is they are often leveraged against the preoccupations of the linguistic turn, specifically its interests in language, consciousness and ideology, and in the critical reading methodologies of deconstruction and psychoanalysis (Leys 2011: 441; Bennett 2010).

The reader of affect theory, my focus here, quickly discovers it is a broad church (Blackman and Venn 2010; La Caze and Lloyd 2011; Gorton 2007). While there are shared interests, the political theorists Ruth Leys discusses in 'The Turn to Affect: A Critique' (2011) – for example, Brian Massumi (2002), William Connolly (2002), Nigel Thrift (2004) – subscribe to ideas of non-signifying, autonomic action that do not square with the historicised and structural notions of affect that inform the writings of feminist theorists such as Sara Ahmed (2014), Lauren Berlant (2008 and 2011) and Lisa Blackman (2012). Given this, it is important to note that terms such as 'the affective turn' (Clough 2007), though common and useful, can skate over important internal differences within this field if applied too broadly.

Studies of emotion have been central to key classical and modern works of scholarly inquiry, including Plato (385–380 BCE), Aristotle (1354, 1447), Descartes (1649), Hobbes (1651) and Darwin (1872), but what is known as the affective turn has quite a specific genealogy. Charting the recent interest in affect, Melissa Gregg and Gregory J. Seigworth locate early inquiries with Sigmund Freud and Baruch Spinoza. However, they suggest that 'undoubtedly the watershed moment for the most recent resurgence of interest and intrigue regarding affect and theories of affect came in 1995 when two essays – one by Eve Kosofsky Sedgwick and Adam Frank ('Shame in the Cybernetic Fold') and one by Brian Massumi ('The Autonomy of Affect') – were published' (2010: 5) (both theorists I discuss here). Gregg and Seigworth suggest that these two essays underpin the two major strands of contemporary affect theory. Sedgwick and Frank emphasise a psychobiological approach, drawing from the work of Silvan Tomkins, while Massumi, drawing from neurobiology and philosophy, anchors his 'immanent affect' in the writings of Gilles Deleuze and Baruch Spinoza. In these definitions, affect is something that operates independently of or through the human, rather than as a property of human personality or relation (Deleuze and Guattari 2000: 470; Tomkins 2008: 656).

There has been a lot of critical writing on the division of affect and emotion from both inside and outside affect theory (Shouse 2005; Barnwell 2018). Unpacking these variations is not the aim of this book; rather I am concerned with how an interest in affect anchors specific shifts in social science methodologies. *Critical Affect* focuses on how and why critical interventions from the mid-1990s onward use affect to pursue an argument about what kinds of truth-telling matter. Affect theory, influenced by Deleuze, Spinoza, Tomkins, Sedgwick and Massumi, but also by Fredric Jameson's 'waning of affect' (1984) and Raymond Williams's 'structures of feeling' (1976), has become increasingly popular since the mid-1990s, sweeping the social sciences and humanities. Its influence can be seen across a diverse range of disciplines. With varying motivations and aims, much of this work champions affect theory for its focus on contagious forces that have productive political effects but defy human-centred intervention. With this intellectual shift away from causality and cognition in many cases comes a stated departure from critical and social scientific methods. *Critical Affect* seeks to slow down this shift and question both its logic and implications. In doing this, it offers us the opportunity to think about how we work with the concept of affect, as well as how we conceive of theoretical and methodological innovation more broadly.

Troubles with Truth-telling in Public and in Scholarship

As the first thing the reader reads, yet the last thing the writer writes, an introduction often masks a period of coalescing and uncertainty with the clarity of hindsight. But the truth of a project's evolution is often less organised and precise. An intellectual exploration, though perhaps considered, methodical and already informed with a unique signature, may not always be aware of its own impetus or goal. As Rebecca Solnit writes in her book about the social life of stories, *The Faraway Nearby* (2013), 'We think we tell stories, but stories often tell us' (4). Questions about where an argument originates and how it works are central to this book, and thus by way of introduction it seems appropriate to give a brief account of how the motivations and direction of this particular project developed.

When I began writing this book it was to be about memoir and truth-telling. I was fascinated by public arguments about what makes a story true and what is socially accepted as evidence in different contexts. My questions were about the everyday methods readers use to decide what is valuable or genuine in literary representations and in public life. For example, if someone transgresses the rules of genre, perhaps using non-fiction to present a fiction, why does it attract moral outrage in some cases and public applause in others? Why are facts important to people in only some instances? Furthermore, how does society deal with its conflicts about what verifies a truth? These were the questions that initially inspired me.

However, when I started to think about my own methods – forms of sociological reading – my focus took an unexpected turn. The very 'genre panic' I was examining in public life was just as central to existing conversations about methodology in the social sciences and humanities. Rather than clarifying the question of how people determine what is true, I found that debates about scholarly methods, even at the cutting edge of interdisciplinary work, were also governed by questions about what should and should not qualify as an authentic account. At conferences and in hallway conversations I was directed again and again to affect theory as a space to pursue my questions about emotion and truth-telling. But in this field I found similar adjudications about whether a story should, first and foremost, have emotional resonance or a verifiable foundation, or about whether we should be more interested in observing the pragmatic, concrete affects of public discourse or unearthing the politics that underpin particular forms of rhetoric. Rather than offering a critical take on these oppositions the literature on affect and methods seemed to present a choice: to stay with the old interest in truth and representation or go with the new interest in emotion and ontology. But what about all the things that fall between? What do we do with the inconsistencies and contradictions that threaten to unhinge the representational practices we rely upon to make life, with all its irresolvable complexities, workable? This question was further complicated, rather than resolved, by the proposals for new methods I read, even when they claimed to know the way forward.

My response to arguments against critique was an intuitive one. To say that critique is out of date because it is suspicious and driven to demystify shonky rhetoric seemed to sit oddly with a post-9/11 landscape where people are targeted for unjust reasons and laws quietly change to abet this, and even more so, in the 'post-truth' era, where day to day we have to sift real from fake news. Similarly, along with colleagues and peers, I find myself in regular battle with the economic structures that surround the production of knowledge in the contemporary academy, as new sets of untransparent figures produced by even less transparent metrics underpin swift policy changes and trigger profound implications, especially for vulnerable students and untenured staff. In these contexts, where the structures that govern our lives are both changeable and opaque, critical hermeneutics does not read as a method for a bygone age or one without affective complexity.

When it comes to making sense of daily life, the troubles of truth-telling and representation seem just as vital. In our everyday dealings we struggle with how best to represent ourselves in a way that is true to our sense of self, but also intelligible to others. We downplay or omit things in certain contexts but emphasise these same attributes in other forums. Similarly, when we explain our work to people, the focus of what we do, the example we choose to give, is slightly different depending on who is asking, where and when. There is not one clearly prescribed, fail-safe way to give account. Our words and actions are shaped and edited in a volatile social arena where the very determinants that guide us – rules and conventions about what is proper and preferred – are also in flux. Yet, in a fascinating complication, we pursue an accurate and reliable way of finding and telling the truth nonetheless. Even as we participate in the changing demands of social life, we desire, and often need, a foundational explanation that sets things out with clear identities and relational patterns, like chemicals in a periodic table with known properties and reactions.

The critical descriptions of critique I read seemed to reduce these ongoing concerns with transparency and truth-telling in ways that work against rather than toward a more inclusive and ecological way of practising theory. Several critics of the critique of critique have noted this already (Best 2017; Fassin 2017; Friedman 2017; McDonald 2018). But the chastening of past efforts is by no means specific to the current turn. Thus I became interested in how and why this practice of 'turning' recurs. What is at stake in performing methodological innovation as a mode of generational succession, or stark division? In the rush to carve out a place for originality, to say that the world presents us with unprecedented problems, do we sometimes overlook the deep roots and continuities of such concerns? Thus while my inquiry began as an interest in public truth-telling it extended into arguments within the social sciences and humanities about how to engage with knowledge in ordinary life. It considers how and why we choose to put down or pick up methods and what falls out of view if we turn too sharply.[6]

Looking Closely At How We Make Methodological Distinctions

This book takes a particular moment – the ontological turn – as its focus, but it is more broadly about the ethics of how we practise and frame theoretical innovation. It aims to both acknowledge and confront our desire for narrative coherence, or for the identities of methods to be fixed and recognisable. What is at stake in the way we read? Why do we scrutinise and obsess over genealogies and causes, or motivations and hidden agendas? Why do we need to make sense of things and to define what is sensible? As narrative theorist Maria Tamboukou explains, in academic analysis we have long desired the 'components of coherence' – 'linearity, completeness, and thematic or moral closure' (2011: 4). However, such intellectual tidiness can also challenge genuinely curious and inclusive thought. When researchers become 'obsessed with identifying these components [. . .] they inevitably suppress or ignore "narrative phenomena" that do not present the attributes of coherence' (4). Wedded to a prescribed form, the critic risks circumscribing intellectual possibilities on many levels: 'analytically (what we can find), cognitively (what we can know), epistemologically (how do we know what we think we know), but also ethically and politically (who gets excluded, and to what effect, from such an approach)' (4). When we commit to a certain set of assumptions about how something is, what its essential elements must be, it is as though we cannot see alternatives or variations. Questions or anomalies that threaten to unsettle the coherence of an answer are either edited out or unconsciously masked. Of course, such editorial and scope-narrowing processes are important and necessary – perhaps even unavoidable. But given the gravity of their effects, they call for a certain level of reflection. Following Tamboukou, my study draws out the risk and ethical tensions involved in determining the rules, identities and capacities of genres. What becomes of the anomalies and contradictions that disturb order? What produces and sustains the divisions that lend identities their form?

At times I use the terms genre and method interchangeably or for a similar purpose. Often within the proposals I discuss claims about the identity of forms pertain to the process of producing them and to the effects they in turn produce. For example, the process of writing a creative short story as academic research is a method, a way of analysing and representing the social world, that is seen to be creative and to incorporate emotion. Similarly, the story itself is thought to have a more affective impact because it is a creative genre. Beyond this, both terms – method and genre – are used to differentiate or to describe something discrete and recognisable, to highlight familiar contours or limits that define and identify.

While method is a more common way to think about form in the social sciences, genre, though often spoken of in terms of literary texts, can also be understood as a sociological phenomenon. The term itself derives from the French word for gender and thus at its very origins speaks to social acts of division and classification that carry great political and ethical consequence. Even in studies of literature, its social nature is often mentioned. John Frow, for instance, describes genre as 'a shared convention with a social force' (2006: 102). Mikhail Bakhtin, often noted as the forefather of genre studies, was interested in how genres, both literary and 'extra-literary', evolve in dialogue with the authors and audiences (1986). Following him, studies of rhetorical genre also extend the concept of literary genres to emphasise genres' socio-cultural functions. In this work, genre is conceived as any space where shared literacies and conventions can be read and practised (see Devitt 2004; Miller 1984).

Referring directly to genre as an authenticating practice, Fredric Jameson notes that genres are 'social contracts between a writer and a specific public whose function is to specify the proper use of a particular cultural artefact' (1981: 106). In life, the public act of marking out what belongs, or as Jameson says, what is 'proper' to a certain grade or order, literally governs whether someone or something can 'fit in'. This contract or convention is directly involved in setting out the terms of social inclusion and exclusion. As Phillip Vannini and J. Patrick Williams explain in *Authenticity in Culture, Self, and Society* (2009), authenticity, one of our most desired forms of cultural capital, operates in these terms, as 'a set of qualities that people in a particular time and place have come to agree represent an ideal or exemplar' (3). But what happens to those that do not possess this set of qualities? Can someone or something be authentic if their particular make-up does not 'fit in'? And if not, what kind of mechanisms and practices does this exclusion generate?

Unpacking these questions across *Critical Affect*, I draw from Bernhard Schlink's meditation on what is at stake in making choices about forms of representation. For Schlink, the question of 'which genre?' is not only about genre preference, it is about maintaining coherence. Schlink argues that what 'lies behind the idea that some events may not be fictionalised or may only be fictionalised while remaining true to the facts is not about the genre, not about documentation versus fiction [. . .] It is about authenticity in a fuller sense' (2009: 119). The terms by which a life story comes to be verified involve a social process of authentication which *is* about genre and *is* about documentation versus fiction, but not as self-evident, static structures. What qualifies as authentic in 'a fuller sense' is liable to social rules, but also to the fickleness of these rules and sometimes to their transgression. What is true, in terms of being socially verified or authentic, is not confined to one genre of truth – historical, empirical or emotional – its narrative may draw from all of these and many other forms of verification in paradoxical, yet workable ways. In this sense, debates about fact and fiction point to underlying social conflicts about authorship and propriety. The trouble is not simply *how* a story is told, but by whom and when and for what purpose. This is just one way that representation and ontology remain entangled. In concert with existing work on the categorising and qualifying processes of public life, I examine how scholars negotiate methodological codes that define the very structures by which they can think and write, as well as what happens to that which is held outside of these domains or provokes their boundaries.

A Return to Close Reading

Because this study is about how we classify and use methods, I have thought a lot about method and realise both the difficulty and responsibility of being clear about one's own methodology. My considerations here are guided by Avery F. Gordon's meditation on sociological inquiry in *Ghostly Matters: Haunting and the Sociological Imagination* (2008). 'How', she asks, 'can our critical language display a reflexive concern not only with the objects of our investigation but also with the ones who investigate? What methods and forms of writing can foreground the conditions under which the facts and the real story are produced?' (24). Gordon does not claim to finally resolve these questions, but neither does she ignore their ethical importance or the need to address them. Indeed, the choice of method Gordon makes is very important in terms of my study of scholarly practice. As I will show across the chapters of this book, there is a current insistence that to tease out the nuances of experience and engage with common truths and beliefs we must discard the truth-seeking motivations of psychoanalytic, deconstructive and new historicist readings to take up new, affect-oriented, experimental practices. But for Gordon, it is these existing methods, psychoanalysis in particular, that can register what falls out of sight when we try to solve the problems of representation by replacing one method with another.

In Gordon's account, the tensions that unsettle a narrative's coherence can never be finally left behind. The unresolved 'ghostly matter' that is excluded from a genre, or a history, or a family – its slips and secrets and inconsistencies – continues to structure and haunt new forms. 'In order to write about [these] invisibilities and hauntings', Gordon argues, 'requires attention to what is not seen, but is nonetheless powerfully real; requires attention to what appears dead, but is nonetheless powerfully alive; requires attention to what appears to be in the past, but is nonetheless powerfully present [...]' (42). Similarly intrigued by what directs, but also disturbs, our preferences and focus, I draw influence from reading practices that look closely at the architecture of an argument. This book features more close-reading than is currently fashionable, but in doing so it attempts to stay close to the arguments of which it is critical and to register the intimate mode of attention Gordon finds in poststructural methods. Following Gordon, my approach tries to recognise the value of existing traditions and questions, but also to resist assuming that one method can finally remedy the apparent failures of another. As with Gordon's sociology, I am interested in the representational and ethical challenges that are inherent to *all* methods, or efforts to account for social life.

In terms of method, Barbara Johnson serves as another inspiring mentor with her 'attention to what is not seen, but is nonetheless powerfully real', and her efforts to understand how difference works. Johnson's deconstructive, close reading practice does not just discard troubled arguments as failed or wrong. Rather, it examines how polemical opinions can be animated and extended by their own misjudgements and contradictions. Johnson argues that when we look closely at things that seem to be at war, we see that their conflict often stems from deep-seated, shared and internal struggles rather than radical, external differences. 'The differences *between* entities', she explains, 'are shown to be based on a repression of differences *within* entities. But the way in which a text differs from itself is never simple: it has a certain rigorous contradictory logic whose effects can, up until a point, be read' (1980 x–xi). Using this mode of analysis, genres are not simply compared; their very difference and make-up is questioned. We are driven to ask: why do we invest in the truth of the story? How did we fill in gaps in evidence and logic? What, in sum, is at stake when we decide which information is vital, simply a mistake or an anomaly? These are the questions *Critical Affect* pursues.

The book is divided into five chapters. Chapter 1, Enduring Divisions, introduces recent critical debates about method and affect by illuminating their links to long-running, interdisciplinary discussions about the ethics of representation. The complex conflict between the truth-values of fact and fiction have been centre stage in both public and academic debates about how to represent social life. By mapping this field for the reader, Chapter 1 presents the current debate about affect and method as only the latest iteration of an enduring conflict over how to access and articulate the dynamic and entangled truths of social life. The chapter then shows how our efforts to address this clash have been even further mired by the rush to elevate fact or fiction rather than posing the question of genre more generally. The current proposal presents a provocative chance to re-examine the terms of this ongoing conflict, as scholars work through, with, and against claims that creative methods can engage with the flux of affect but that critical methods are too obsessed with evidence and revelation.

Delving deeper into current debates, the middle three chapters offer a sustained case study of the turn away from critical methods. My analysis of this popular and expanding interdisciplinary field focuses on how it navigates and informs discourses about the value of methods. As I will explain, these influential proposals grapple with their own internal divisions while also pursuing an inclusive and generous practice. Its proponents argue that if social scientists break from abstract, academic scrutiny they could engage the flux of lived experience in a way that is both ethical and authentic. I have chosen to focus on thinkers and texts that are commonly cited as influential. Analysing key theoretical, methodological and practical exemplars, these three chapters examine whether such a shift can alleviate critical exclusion, or if it continues to circumscribe which methods can hold intellectual and practical value. As an extended case study of several stages in the development of an argument, these three chapters also offer insight into how ideas and directives can take hold and even thrive, despite deep internal conflicts, unseen commitments and acts of self-negation. In this current effort to forge methods that can access the real stuff of life, old questions about the nature of evidence, the propriety of disciplines and the social value of intellectual work are revived.

After introducing the genealogy and current status of the turn from critique, Chapter 2, Evidence in Flux, analyses the directives of two of its most influential advocates, Eve Kosofsky Sedgwick (1997) and Bruno Latour (2004). Paying particular attention to the stated concerns and motivations of these foundational arguments, my analysis considers how these theorists' own methods of verification – weaving together felt and factual truths – challenge the assumption that critical and affect-oriented forms of inquiry are at odds. The chapter also gives insight into how the paranoid atmospheres surrounding the Cold War, the AIDS crisis and the Cultural Wars influenced the timbre and response of theory across the turn of the century. It locates a lingering suspicion – the very sentiment that is marked as no longer vital – in the turn against critique and argues that this recuperation calls for further attention.

Influenced by the arguments discussed in the previous chapter, as well as by Brian Massumi's 'The Autonomy of Affect' (1995, 2002), critics such as Nigel Thrift (2007) and John Law (2004) argue that creative genres of representation, such as fiction and performance, are more affective and can thus access the visceral truth of experience better than scientific and critical methods. Analysing the proposals of Thrift and Law, Chapter 3, The Crisis of 'Non-Representation', explores why certain methods are deemed to be more creative than others, and therefore more in touch with embodied experience. Highlighting some of the persistent tensions in these method proposals, I argue that we should reconsider the social purchase of critical attention and what Paul Ricœur called 'the hermeneutics of suspicion'. To do this, the chapter locates an intriguing parallel between a public fascination with conspiracy culture and secrecy and affect theory's concerns about unseen agencies and atmospheres. Indeed, the bestselling novels and most watched television programmes of our times present popular representations of 'the hermeneutics of suspicion'. Read in social context, the divisions between critical and creative or common forms of attention become less resolute. Critique can be seen as socially impelled rather than socially redundant.

Chapter 4, Ordinary Paranoia, looks deeper into the fascinating 'paranoia paradox' that has emerged in the previous two chapters. Critics argue that critique is out of touch with social reality because it has become invested with the wrong motives, namely suspicions about hidden agencies and inequalities. Yet, as the previous chapter demonstrates, very similar reading practices are lively and abundant in everyday life. Following on from the theoretical and method directives discussed so far, this chapter focuses on Kathleen Stewart's ethnography, *Ordinary Affects* (2007). Explicitly framed as a turn against what Sedgwick terms 'paranoid reading', Stewart's evocative ethnography ironically describes a hyper-vigilant public. Drawing together quotidian and academic methods of interpretation, this chapter foregrounds the value of the 'hermeneutics of suspicion' as a dynamic, everyday method for navigating shifting social structures, including the changeable structures, rules and values of methods themselves. It shows that critical attention can be intuitive and creative: the very means by which people anticipate the future and make unsure decisions in real time.

The fifth and final chapter, The Life of Genre, draws out what is at stake when we recuperate conflicts between creative and critical methods and social and scholarly modes of interpretation. The preceding chapters demonstrate that such divisions, when examined closely, always unravel. Here I ask why, given these blurring edges, we insist on thinking about method along such oppositional lines and what are the consequences for the ethics of social inquiry? Drawing from writings by Bernhard Schlink and Barbara Johnson on the dangers of polemical thinking and rationalisation, this final chapter evaluates both the quandaries and potential of current debates about affect and critique. I conclude that rather than trying to decide which is the 'right' mode to engage with social life, as if method were an external lens, we might think about our methods as part of the very social flux that we seek to address. In this light, 'paranoid reading' can be seen as an immanent response to the instability of social structures, rather than a defunct method of decades past. Concluding the argument, this chapter aerates divisions in current methodological debates and re-enlists critique as a valuable method for engaging with questions about affect, ontology and social transformation.

Across the course of these five chapters I argue that the pursuit of truth – the question of its form and the conditions of its verification – is both more complex and dynamic than a strict division between critical interpretation and creative intuition will allow. I explore how hermeneutic processes are, as Paul Ricœur has argued, not simply positive *or* negative (1970).Verifying practices that appear to uphold the rules of genre – whether it is the drive behind an academic argument or the evidence that a memory rests upon or a person's justification for their political preferences – are often revising and bending these conventions in fascinating ways. This book then, overall, shows how questions of representation remain crucial for the ontological turn. It asks not how we can break from the blinders of scholarly methods to see the raw realities of social life, but rather aims to rethink the composition of authorship, veracity and genres of interpretation in a way that contests the propriety of these spheres. At the crux of *Critical Affect* is a foundational, socio-logical and ethical question about how we decide what is valuable and true, as well as an exploration of the peculiar means by which these choices are often defended.

1

Enduring Divisions

This chapter introduces recent critical debates about method and affect by illuminating their links to long-running, interdisciplinary discussions about the ethics of representation. The complex conflict between the truth-values of fact and fiction have been central in both public and academic debates about how to represent social life, from rifts between positivist sociologists and social novelists in nineteenth-century Paris, to controversies over New Journalism's fictionalised reports in the 1970s, to the 'crisis of representation' about writing ethnographies in the 1980s, to scandals about the truth-value of embellished autobiographies in the 2000s. All of these cases reveal a provocative anxiety about how writers – of various genres – should represent experiences and events in a way that is both verified *and* resonant with the actual dimensions of subjective accounts.

By mapping a selective genealogy of the fact/fiction conundrum here, I show how the current debate about affect and method refigures an enduring conflict over how to represent the mutable and diverse truths of social life. The chapter is structured to lead readers through present and past debates about the politics of method, where similar concerns about how to tell the truth can be seen to shift in structure and terminology across multiple fields, but also maintain a provocative continuity and irresolution. Via this mapping, I argue that our efforts to determine the most authentic mode of representation have been consistently challenged by the need to privilege one genre over another, or vice versa, rather than opening up the question of how genres are determined. In each instance, however, the capacities of particular modes of representation, while assumed to be fixed, remain difficult to pin down.

The current proposal that scholars should use creative methods to engage with the flux of affect because critical methods are outmoded presents a chance to re-examine the terms of the 'two cultures' and to explore how current debates refigure enduring concerns about social science methodologies. Looking at what appears to be a set of new questions within a rich cultural history reorients the trajectory of theoretical innovation away from a very linear idea of intellectual progress and recognises the intimate entanglement of past and present questions. Less focus on novelty is important because, as we will see, by presenting each methodological approach as radically new we risk obscuring a history of nuanced insights that emerge from previous discussions about truth and veracity. Through this lens we can open up queries about the enduring structures of methodological thinking, rather than only focusing on the pursuit of new methods. With this less censorious approach it is possible to unpack the insights of what may appear to be an error or an impasse in intellectual work.

In the following chapters I will closely examine how this division dissolves in a way that highlights the affective and dynamic potential of critical reading and attention. Here, my aim is to track how an initial division is authored. While the preference for particular scholarly narratives is articulated by disciplinary structures, it is crucial to highlight that these structures themselves are narratives that are created and maintained. Therefore, when we analyse how scholars contend with disciplinary identities, it is vital to consider how they participate in their construction, that is how interventions *into* social inquiry define the terms of a problem in the very act of leveraging solutions.

The 'Two Cultures'

Just as the politics of authenticity challenges social decisions about what is and is not true, it influences the identity of academic methods, both within and between disciplinary circles. In the academy, the division of affective and factual truths is traditionally expressed in what C. P. Snow termed the 'two cultures' ([1959] 1998), widely understood as the partition between scientific and humanist disciplines or 'the confrontation of cold rationality and the culture of feeling' (Lepenies 1988: 1). When Snow first delivered his famous Rede lecture in 1959, he raised concerns about the siloed knowledges of the sciences and the humanities, and their intellectual suspicion of one another. As a chemist *and* a novelist, Snow was well positioned to notice the cultural gulf between his fellow scientists and literary intellectuals, neither of whom, he argued, was well versed in the fields of the other. Snow saw this as the fault of the Victorian British education system and argued that it would leave the educated ill-equipped to face challenges requiring a synthesis of knowledge ([1959] 1998). In an exemplification of the very rift Snow attempted to identify, man of letters F. R. Leavis mounted a sharp rebuttal, arguing against the idea that scientific thought could lead the way to bridging the divide (and denying Snow's literary talent) (Leavis [1962] 2013). As a result, much of the discussion after Snow's lecture missed his point and quibbled over whether the sciences or the humanities would be the field to solve the 'two cultures' dilemma.

As Daniel Cordle explains in *Postmodern Postures: Literature, Science and the Two Cultures Debate* (1999), the 'science wars of the 1990s showcased the stubborn resilience of the two cultures rift and further polarised the disciplines. The division was revived, and slightly refigured, when the physicist, Alan Sokal, staged a hoax. He submitted a pseudo-scientific paper (1996a) to the cultural studies journal *Social Text* to prove that the humanities would 'publish an article liberally salted with nonsense if (a) it sounded good and (b) it flattered the editors' ideological preconceptions' (Sokal 1996b). With this hoax, Sokal expressed and exacerbated a pre-existing concern, in this case about why we regard certain genres such as scientific stories as essentially authentic. Sokal set up boundaries of representational propriety around the field of quantum physics in response to social scientists, particularly those in science and technology studies, writing about the construction of truth and error in science labs. Rather than seeing all genres as, in different ways, truth-making, Sokal claimed that cultural theorists, using pithy writing styles, obfuscate the facts of science in a way that scientists writing reports do not. Critical theory, in his eyes, plaits science with quackery and poetry in disregard for the rigour of facts.

On the other side of the debate, postmodern cultural theorists chided scientists for their unreflexive positivism, insisting that the empirical verification of facts, always mediated through a very human set of prejudices, must be a relative and subjective social construction. This critique drew attention to the often unquestioned authority of science but sometimes reduced science, particularly its effectiveness and diversity, in the very same way that Sokal refused to engage with the complex, plural and contested fields within the social sciences and humanities. In an intellectual war over which disciplinary genre offers a more truthful insight, the underlying question of how and why genres are relied upon to transparently produce or grant access to particular truths remained mostly unexamined on both sides (see also Parsons 2003 and Ashman and Barringer 2000). If the science wars unveiled something, it was surely just how *un*sure we remain about the nature of fact and interpretation or the relation of truth and genre. However, the discourse surrounding this scandal reductively split scholars, based on what disciplinary genres they use, into those who verify knowledge with 'facts' and those who verify knowledge with 'values'. Academic work in this long-running polemic is routinely thought to exclusively address either objective *or* subjective realities, facts *or* fictions, natural *or* cultural phenomena.

'The two cultures', as an enduringly productive convention, also inform the identities of and relationship between the *social* sciences and humanities. Though driven by common questions, social scientists are presumed to analyse real people and literary scholars to analyse representational characters. Of course, history is rife with instances of inquiry that defy this division of labour. Sigmund Freud's psychoanalytic works, for instance, blur this distinction constantly, drawing from canonical and obscure fiction, ancient history, scientific studies, patients' testimonies, letters, myths and dreams to inform his theories. Similarly, Walter Benjamin's Marxist work on the industrialisation of Paris enlists the poetry of Charles Baudelaire, almost as reportage, to capture the nuances of the sensual, everyday response to changing social configurations ([1939] 1983; 1968c). However, despite this counter-history, an academic division of emotional versus verifiable truths noticeably continues to inform disciplinary identities, conservative and radical alike.

The aesthetics of this division, constructing social science as analytical and literature as intuitive, are routinely reiterated even by unexpected voices. A writer such as E. L. Doctorow, for instance, not positioned in the academy and famous for his genre-bending historical fictions (Henry 1997; Strout 1980), ascribes facts to social inquiry and emotion to literary inquiry. In *False Documents* (1977), Doctorow challenges the privileging of scientific over fictional truth. He argues that the division between emotional and verifiable truths is a recent and flawed construction. However, it is the hierarchy, not the *division* of value, which Doctorow challenges. His description of genres plainly utilises the language Snow deemed reductive in his critique of disciplinary insularity. 'Sociologists and social psychologists', Doctorow explains, 'not only make communion with *facts* but in addition display the *scientific* method of dealing with them. The tale told by the social scientists, the counsel given, is *nonspecific, collated, and subject to verification*' (1977: 231, emphasis added). Literary scholars, conversely, deal with 'fiction', a '*not entirely rational* means of discourse', and deliver different counsel than that of social science (231, emphasis added). The 'complex understandings' of literature are '*indirect, intuitive, and non-verbal*': they 'arise from the words of the story, and by a ritual transaction [. . .] instructive *emotion* is generated in the reader [. . .]' (231, emphasis added). Couched in these terms, Doctorow registers sociology as an objective science dealing with life and literary studies as an emotive engagement with fiction. Even in a treatise written to demystify the mythology of genre by an author renowned for twisting form, the legacy of the 'two cultures' is surprisingly robust.

Similarly, in academic circles, this division persists even in more radical and experimental spheres, where the aim may be to break free from convention and structure. I turn now to examine the 'critique of critique' – to show how the terms of its arguments reiterate a 'two cultures' structure that, in this case, finds an impasse between critique and affect. By examining such arguments, we can gain insight into how new logics retread well-worn paths, and reflect on why discussions about the future of social science methods are so often built around an oppositional rift and a methodological corrective.

The Critique of Critique

In the past few decades, scholars within both the social sciences and humanities have expressed their fatigue and dissatisfaction with critique (Latour 2004; Sedgwick 1997; Felski 2015; Barad, in Dolphijn and van der Tuin 2012; Aagaard 2018) – this position has been variously called the 'critique of critique' (Boland 2019), 'anti-critique' (Noys 2010; McDonald 2018) and 'post-critique' (Best 2017). Critique is of course a very diverse orientation or method, practised in many different ways across myriad disciplines and eras. In the arguments I refer to here, the target is more selective: 'critique' stands in for schools of thought and modes of reading that were influenced by poststructuralism, most specifically deconstruction, new historicism, postcolonial theory and queer and feminist theories of the 1980s and 1990s. These methods are thought to be united by a focus on revealing hidden subplots and biases – such as a queer reading that finds a homoerotic narrative running through what seems to be a heteronormative romance novel, or a postcolonial approach which uncovers imperialist motives in a purportedly inclusive 'multicultural' migration policy. Rather than exploring the history and diversity of critical approaches, critics seize 'critique' at a particular moment in time, as an approach that is thought to have become dominant but perfunctory in its focus on ulterior workings, structural causes or hidden agencies, and to pose an obstacle to pursuing genuine knowledge and engagement. Scholars in literary studies, most prominently Eve Kosofsky Sedgwick (1997) and, later, Rita Felski (2015), have also focused on what they see to be the limited emotional range of critique and argue that critical reading forces both scholars and readers to feel negative emotions such as paranoia and suspicion towards texts, rather than positive responses such as love or enchantment. As an alternative to critique, some of these arguments propose a range of 'post-critical' methods and reading practices, which are seen to be more capable of reaching the dynamic and affective aspects of contemporary life.

Because key texts of the critique of critique and turn to affect are analysed in detail in the following chapters, here I introduce central arguments within the literature and unpack their potential implications for how we practise social science. This broader account will demonstrate how the identities and limitations of genres are drawn and fixed in a way that may actually work against a more generous engagement with the dynamic and entangled life of methods. However, as I will show in later chapters, these polemic fixings never quite hold, and for this reason the critique of critique offers a rich ground upon which to reconsider the politics of method.

In a field such as the sociology of literature, where scholars explicitly work across the divide, the turn away from critique is being described not just as a new avenue for the field, but as a remedy to the 'two cultures' division. Mapping the field in the 1970s, Diana Laurenson and Alan Swingewood claimed that agonistic disciplinary cultures hampered intellectual growth: 'The sociological study of literature has not developed, either in terms of its theory or in its methods of analysis, but has remained in some kind of limbo, suspended between literature as literature and sociology as social science' (vii). On one side, they explained, there are 'those who believe that social science is simply the study of *facts*', and on the other, 'those for whom literature is a unique subjective experience which defies scientific analysis' (vii). In the 1980s , surveying the field again, Priscilla Parkhurst Ferguson et al. proclaimed that the 'most basic boundary line divides literary studies and social science' and that this 'fundamental opposition between the two determines work in the sociology of literature more than might be supposed for such avowedly interdisciplinary work' (1988: 421; see also Desan et al. 1989).

Taking the pulse of the sociology of literature in 2010, James F. English notes that the professional stereotyping with which Snow charged 'men of science' and 'men of letters' still thrives in the academy. In this bleak landscape, he writes, literary studies' conception of sociology maligns the sociologist's project as akin to, if not in cahoots with, the economic quantification, restructuring and retrenchment of intellectual work in the humanities. English cautions that 'literary scholars seem less able than ever to map themselves on the higher-educational landscape without reference to that presumed fault line [. . .]' between social science and the humanities (2010: xiii, xiv– xv). Humanities scholars, he adds, hold a 'view of sociology, and of the social sciences in general, as allied with the hegemony of numbers, and as a discipline decisively favored, over and against the humanities, by the despised new managers of higher education' (xiii).

But the resilience of this divisive structure is also evident in the way English figures novel approaches in opposition to critique, and casts the turn to post-critical methods as the way forward for the sociology of literature. At first the problem he describes is structural, exacerbated by economic rationalisation, but then, as the argument unfolds, there is a shift of focus to critique and its dominance as the main problem, and one that requires a methodological corrective. English first argues that it is under the banner of critique that sociological work on literature has flourished despite institutional constraints:

> Wherever [critical theorists] might be located on the map of named and recognized subfields – postcolonial studies, queer theory, new historicism – their shared disciplinary mission was to coordinate the literary with the social: to provide an account of literary texts and practices by reference to the social forces of their production, the social meanings of their formal particulars, and the social effects of their circulation and reception. (viii)

However, when English comes to conclude his summary the determinants of his argument shift. There is a leap from the success of critique – in all its diversity – as one of these 'stealthily advancing' unions of social and literary matters to not only a diagnosis of critique's exhaustion, but also the positioning of critique as the wedge between sociology and literary studies.

> [W]hatever its reputational and nomenclatural fates may have been since the late 1970s and early 1980s, the sociology of literature has not actually receded. Instead, it has become partner to a great many significant and innovative projects that are no less sociological for bearing other labels than 'the sociology of literature.' It has stealthily advanced on many fronts and seems now [. . .] to be arriving at a point of especially rich potential as both sociology and literary studies turn toward new, more rigorously 'descriptive' or 'pragmatic' approaches, rejecting the long-dominant paradigm of critique that has governed and limited the previous history of their encounters. (xii)

In the space of these few sentences, English shifts from exploring the structural and intellectual pressures on interdisciplinary research to celebrating new methods which are leveraged against a prohibitive critique. Where he sets out to question the rift between sociology and literary studies, English begins to re-anchor a division, setting up critique as the antagonist to 'new' methods, and the future of the field, in this case.[1]

This oligarchical characterisation of critique, paired with a diagnosis of its waning relevance, is a common feature in critiques of critique that argue for new methods. Very rarely are actual examples of critique cited or analysed. Rather 'Critique' features almost as a character in its own right, a malevolent Iago grasping onto power and infecting scholars and students with suspicious logic. Similarly 'new methods' are heralded as a much-needed, positive antidote to the negativity of critique, but are also quite thinly outlined.[2]

Several arguments against critique repeat this structure of conversion. For example, Eve Kosofsky Sedgwick champions 'reparative reading' over 'paranoid reading' (1997), which Lauren Berlant has termed her 'antidote to the hermeneutics of suspicion' (Berlant 2011: 122–3). Stephen Best and Sharon Marcus offer 'surface reading' as an alternative to Louis Althusser's 'symptomatic' reading (2009). Other methodological manifestos, including Nigel Thrift's 'non-representational theory' (2007), Michael Warner's 'uncritical reading' (2004) and Rachael Ablow's 'affective reading' (2010), also call for alternatives to critique that are essentially positive. All of these method proposals share a similar structure, seeking to make up for the ethical and explanatory failings of critical methods with novel forms of inquiry. In 'Reading with the Grain: A New World in Literary Criticism' (2010), for instance, Timothy Bewes proposes his own notion of 'reading with the grain' as an antidote to Walter Benjamin's suspicious 'reading against the grain'.

---

[1] For a detailed analysis of English's argument see Barnwell (2015).

[2] Mariam Fraser also notices the congruence/conflict between older and recent debates about sociological methods versus 'craftsmanship' (2009). However, interestingly, in the debates she traces about the conflict between sociology and cultural studies (67), poststructuralist critique's creativity is posited as the adversary of sociology's scientism. In the turn discussed in this chapter, the line between adversaries is drawn differently: poststructural schools are grouped *with* the suspicion of Marxist sociology, and positioned against the creativity of aesthetics. The variation of these two accounts, only a few years apart, further highlights the fickleness of boundaries assumed to divide evidentiary and experiential concerns.

Bewes underlines 'the need to outgrow our supposedly Benjaminian habits of reading against the grain – the phrase that functioned as a byword for theoretically informed criticism in the second half of the twentieth century' (4). He contends that 'in its place would appear a reading that suspends judgment, that commits itself, rather, to the *most generous reading possible*' (4).

Picking up this note on generosity, Bruno Latour, a key figure in the critique of critique, frames the departure as an ethical imperative on the premise that critique is ultimately dismissive of people's everyday attachments. Latour diagnoses faith in demystification as bad scholarship and calls for 'a suspension of the critical impulse' in order to 'repair, take care, assemble, reassemble, stitch together' (2010: 4). Firstly, in 'Why Has Critique Run Out of Steam: From Matters of Fact to Matters of Concern' (2004), he opposes the iconoclastic methods of critique to a more generous treatment of matters of concern. Translating this shift into a method in 'The Compositionist Manifesto' (2010), Latour proscribes 'compositionism' as an alternative to what he sees to be Deconstruction's 'destructive' methods. Latour argues that critique has made a career out of denouncing the efficacy of people's values. He asserts that critique's limited 'fact' (positivist) and 'fairy' (poststructuralist) narratives always give the critic the upper hand in unveiling the illusory fetishes of the 'naïve believer' (2005: 238) and have 'had the immense drawback of creating a massive gap between what was felt and what was real' (2010: 4). In 'After Suspicion' (2009), Rita Felski similarly argues that 'suspicion', the term she uses to characterise critique, 'sustains and reproduces itself in a reflexive distrust of common knowledge and an emphasis on the chasm that separates scholarly and lay interpretation' (29). It is, she suggests, a method from which we must 'turn' if we are to 'build better bridges between theory and common sense, between academic criticism and ordinary reading' (31). While arguments such as these hope to open up a plural, inclusive, and ethical practice, they do not engage with the implicit recuperation of disciplinary exclusion – including their demotion of a great many critical and sociological concerns, both past and present – or essentialist notions about the exclusive efficacy of certain genres.

There are also shaky assumptions made about the demands of the political context. Sharon Marcus and Stephen Best's proposal for surface reading, another 'recent [call] for alternatives to critical hermeneutics' (Love 2010: 387), provides an example of this. In their editorial introduction to 'The Way We Read Now' (2009), Best and Marcus argue against 'symptomatic reading', their synonym for critique. This term has its origin in sociology with Louis Althusser's study of Marx [1970] (1979), but Best and Marcus use it to describe a widespread method that they argue was 'popularised by the linguistic turn of the 1970s' and 'the acceptance of psychoanalysis and Marxism as metalanguages' in the humanities. They contend that such approaches are based on the belief that 'what a text means lies in what it does not say' (2009: 1). Best and Marcus argue that this method is not relevant to contemporary political realities, but rather has come to seem 'nostalgic, even utopian' (1–2). Justifying this waning relevance, they contend that:

> Those of us who cut our intellectual teeth on deconstruction, ideology critique, and the hermeneutics of suspicion have often found those demystifying protocols superfluous in an era when images of torture at Abu Ghraib and elsewhere were immediately circulated on the internet; the real-time coverage of Hurricane Katrina showed in ways that required little explication the state's abandonment of its African American citizens; and many people instantly recognized as lies political statements such as 'mission accomplished.' (2)

Best and Marcus argue that because political injustice is now transparent and 'on the surface' we should perform surface readings. They state that one of their aims is to demonstrate that 'to see more clearly does not require that we plumb hidden depths' (18).

The examples Best and Marcus offer to suggest that critical methods, or 'deep readings', are no longer necessary require some attention. In the most basic respect, the political events Marcus and Best argue require 'surface reading': the release of photographs of torture at Abu Ghraib were not transparent until they were made so. Evidence of this corruption made it into the media and online, enabling a 'surface reading' only after it was deliberately brought to the surface by a 'symptomatic' reading of some kind, in this case an official military inquiry leading to the Taguba Report (2004) and the investigative journalism of Seymour M. Hersh for *The New Yorker* (2004). Similarly, the fact that then US President George Bush was re-elected to serve another term in office after he flew the banner stating 'mission accomplished', a slogan that Best and Marcus explain 'many people instantly recognized as lies', suggests it may not be time to dismiss rigorous scrutiny just yet.

Rita Felski, who has established herself as one of the foremost critics of the hermeneutics of suspicion in literary studies (2008, 2009, 2011a, 2011b, 2015), also bases her argument on an assumed consensus that critique has run its course: 'a dawning sense among literary and cultural critics that a shape of thought has grown old' (2008: 1). In a collective pronoun, she argues that demystification is outdated in a world where apparently all is self-evident:

> We know only too well the well-oiled machine of ideology critique, the x-ray gaze of symptomatic-reading, the smoothly rehearsed moves that add up to a hermeneutics of suspicion. Ideas that seemed revelatory thirty years ago – the decentered subject! The social construction of reality! – have dwindled into shop-worn slogans [...] what virtue remains in unmasking when we know full well what lies beneath the mask? (1)

Just as English contends that critique keeps sociology and literary studies apart, Felski claims that critique divides the scholar from social reality. She argues that scholars who practise critique are not truly concerned with revealing the nature of reality, but with the ease and satisfaction drawn from using the well-rehearsed method of revelation itself.

Felski characterises critique with her own summative impression rather than quoting or attending to specific examples. In a later book, she takes the same approach, describing what she calls 'a widespread sensibility and an immediately recognizable shape of thought', and casting 'critique as a genre and an ethos – as a transpersonal and wide-spread phenomenon rather than the brainchild of a few eminent thinkers' (2015: 4). When lined up, the words Felski uses to depict critique in her introduction form an ungenerous portrait. Critique is 'a quintessentially paranoid style' which 'calls for constant vigilance, reading against the grain, assuming the worst-case scenario, and then

rediscovering its own gloomy prognosis in every text' (2008: 3). It is
'a stance of permanent skepticism and sharply honed suspicion', an
'automatism of our own resistance' (3). Though critique 'prides itself
on its exquisite self-consciousness [...] the very adoption of such a
stance is pre-conscious rather than freely-made, choreographed rather
than chosen, determined in advance by the pressure of institutional
demands, intellectual prestige, and the status-seeking of professional
advancement' (4). It 'subordinate[s]' literature and 'haul[s]' it in to
'confirm what the critic already knows' (7). It is a 'style of criticism
[...] propelled by a deep-seated discomfort with everyday language
and thought, a conviction that commonsense beliefs exist only to
be unmasked and found wanting' (13). It is a form of theory that
'requires us to go behind the backs of ordinary persons in order to
expose their beliefs as deluded or delinquent' (13). With this battering
of descriptors, Felski constructs a repellent and duplicitous antagonist.
She argues that the way forward is to embrace more positive and
descriptive forms of reading that allow for a diversity of emotional
engagements.

As we think about the politics of method, it is important to ask:
what is to be gained by offering such an ungenerous and unsubstanti-
ated account of critical work – one which presumes of our peers rote
thinking, if not bad faith? Though they are diverse, implicit in several
of these proposals is the assumption that critique has not and cannot facilitate an engagement with how social values come to verify
facts, how facts come to verify social values, and the complication and
entanglement of these processes. However, from Marx's commodity
fetishism ([1875] 1974) and Émile Durkheim's social facts ([1895 and
1897] 1982 and 1970) to Pierre Bourdieu's symbolic power (1984)
and Robert K. Merton's self-fulfilling prophesies (1948), sociology
has dealt with questions of how social structures and subjectivities
can be *actualised* by projections and desires. In 1928, the sociologists
W. I. Thomas and D. S. Thomas also formulated their famous 'Thomas
theorem' – 'if men define situations as real, they are real in their consequences' – in an effort to understand the productivity of belief and
the very real outcomes of situated knowledges (571–2). The sociological pursuit of facticity, in these traditions, does not simply expose
the falseness of false consciousness, but is interested in how truths are
produced and come to matter, in both senses of the word.

Similarly, deconstruction is not purely destructive but aims to wrest possibilities of meaning from open texts. Though often contrary, Jacques Derrida does not simply declare that reading Rousseau is a waste of time, nor does Paul de Man dismiss the project of Romanticism. These are not wholly negative pursuits. Their readings deal closely and reparatively, though not uncritically, with past works. Railing against deconstruction, Latour asks for 'critical proximity' rather than 'critical difference' (2005: 8), but this is what such close readings already offer by, as Vicki Kirby describes, 'making [themselves] at home in the very logic of [their] opponent's argument and showing how the direction of that argument can comprehend a very different set of implications' (Kirby 2012: 86). Indeed, the careful attention to the primary text in much poststructuralist work is more generous and proximate than, for example, Felski's argument against critique, as cited above, which draws pejorative conclusions without evidence. Even in an ungenerous reading of critique, surely, in keeping with Latour's project to open up which actors contribute to and animate life, such historical precedents – even their suspicion, judgement and criticality – must remain part of the puzzle? What might we learn from previous struggles to navigate the inextricability of facts and values? Do all attachments, we might ask these ancestors, call for reparation? To be generous, must scholars be positive or is being decisive, or even incisive, also a form of care?

Critique and Affect

In the proposals I have discussed so far, critique is set aside voluntarily in pursuit of new methods. But there is also an influential strand of argument within the critique of critique which contends that critical judgement is *by nature* not useful for research on affect. This argument has come to be important in methodological works, such as Nigel Thrift's *Non-Representational Theory* (2007) and John Law's *After Method: Mess as Social Science Research* (2004), which suggest that affective phenomena call for modes of representation such as film, performance or creative writing to capture their essential fluidity. Much has been written about Brian Massumi's highly influential theorisation of affect, including several compelling critiques of its implications for social science and the ethics of representation (Hemmings 2006; Papoulias and Callard 2010; Leys 2011). Rather than repeat these, I revisit Massumi's work to pinpoint two claims that are cited as a rationale for the turn against critique in affect studies: firstly, that affect is pre-cognitive and pre-structural; and secondly, that affect is immune to critique. In his argument we see how the 'two cultures' debate lives on in a refigured form. Where emotion was opposed to reason, Massumi sets affect as the free and fluid other of emotion's rationalised schema. Where critical reading has posed a radical opposition to scientism, Massumi uses a creative reading of neuroscientific findings to frame critique as arid and authoritarian. The content of his arguments is different but the polemic form is the same: a call for new methods is offered as a corrective based on the claim that current methods are inapt.

In his controversial division of emotion and affect (Seyfert 2012; Wetherell 2015), Massumi argues that affect exists outside codification, is resistant to critique and demands new methods of engagement. For Massumi emotions are affect that has been 'pinned down' and defined in words, and thereby rendered static by structure:[3] 'What they [emotions] lose, precisely, is the expression *event* – in favour of structure' (1995: 87). Massumi bases this claim on findings from two neuroscience experiments from the 1980s, known as the 'snowman experiment' (Sturm 1987) and the 'missing half second experiment'.[4] Massumi reads both of these clinical experiments to suggest that people can respond powerfully to events before they cognitively register and describe what is happening. He then takes this finding as evidence that it is the body which processes affect and impels us, and when the conscious mind catches up bringing with it sociological sense-making, affect's

---

[3] Alongside the argument that emotions, as linguistically anchored affects, cannot capture change it is interesting to consider that the etymology of the word 'emotion' suggests movement: the French *émotion* derives from *émouvoir* which means 'to stir up' or 'agitate,' which stems from the Latin *emovere* meaning 'to move out'.

[4] In his account, Massumi does not cite from the original experiment or its lead scientist Benjamin Libet. But accounts of this experiment and related studies can be found in Libet (1979, 1982, 1985). It is interesting to note that, in later years, Libet wrote critically about the ethical implications of his arguments for issues around responsibility and volition in collaboration with philosophers of free will (Libet, with Freeman and Sutherland 1999).

effects are already in motion. Massumi interprets the experiments to mean 'the skin is faster than the word' (Massumi 1995: 85). This, importantly, becomes the basis for his argument about critique's essential inadequacy.

Several critics have pointed out the issues with Massumi's use of dated neuroscientific studies to make claims about the validity of social science methods, while also ignoring decades of research from the sociology of emotions or feminist science studies that challenges the division of body and mind or instinct and cognition (Papoulias and Callard 2010; Leys 2011). But despite these issues, Massumi's theorisation has been widely cited as a rationale for the pursuit of post-critical methods. '[Affect]', he argues, 'is not ownable or recognizable, and is thus resistant to critique' (88). Explaining this point further in an interview, Massumi states that '"[c]ritical" practices aimed at increasing potentials for freedom or for movement are inadequate, because in order to critique something in any definitive way you have to pin it down' (Massumi, in Zournazi 2002: 220). He further contends that this 'pinning down' 'is an almost sadistic enterprise that separates something out, attributes set characteristics to it, then applies a final judgement to it – objectifies it in a mor- alising kind of way [...] I think [critique] loses contact with other more moving dimensions of experience' (220). For Massumi, the primary action of critique is 'judgement' which he argues is not at all useful for working with affect. He writes that '[critique] doesn't allow for other kinds of practices that might not have so much to do with mastery and judgement as with affective connection and abductive participation' (220). Here critique is described as unuse- ful and unethical, and as a method that cannot reach the affective dimensions of social life. His argument offers a clear example of a strong push away from critique based on an assumption that the method can be, ironically, 'pinned down' to a very limited set of aims and functions.

These critiques of critique set up a refigured version of the 'two cultures' where methods and their capacities are opposed and fixed. The aim is initially a generous one – to advocate for more inclusive and ethical modes of representation. But, in doing so, existing modes of inquiry are unnecessarily caricatured and demoted. To counter this reduction, for the remainder of this chapter I put the 'critique of critique' into the context of long-running debates about genre and method. Viewed within this intellectual history we see how a turn to 'the new', or how presenting this issue of competing methods as a novel problem, veils a history of discussions within social science and beyond that have mulled over shared questions about how we can faithfully account for life. In some cases, these previous discussions offer insights into or trouble assumptions that operate within the current debate. Past cases allow us to consider several important questions: is the history of disciplinary and methodological divisions as neat as it appears? Are only some genres or methods prone to problems and ethical issues when it comes to social explanation? And finally, can what are seen to be more creative and emotional modes of writing resonate better with public readerships, or more accurately capture the dynamics of everyday life? What this contextualisation shows us, overall, is that the constitution and reception of genres is very complex and requires a curious mode of attention that is open to the mutability of methods. I turn first to the rise of sociology and its conflicted position between science and literature, then to the 1980s 'crisis of representation' and debates about ethnography, and finally to public responses to the blurring of fact and fiction in narrative journalism and memoir.

An Impure History: 'Blurred Genres' at Social Science's Roots

Histories of the birth of sociology chart the influence of both the sciences and the arts on the discipline's aims. They tell a story about conflict and irresolvable difference, but also one of contagion and overlap, where it becomes much harder to follow a steady, through-running schism (Nisbet 1966; Hawthorn 1976; Lepenies 1988; Mazlish 1989; Heilbron 1995). Instead, the positioning of the line between cultures shifts around because it is drawn and redrawn by the very lives and times of the scholars who work within and across the sciences and the humanities. Where critics of critique often see a stalemate between structural and affective concerns, or between critical and creative methods, there is a long and fascinating history of Trojan horses and treason, and in less sinister terms, a genuine, if sometimes competitive, interest in shared questions. Close attention to the intellectual history unsettles an account of methodological progress where new interventions increasingly open the capacity for more inclusive, creative and unbridled research. Though this is not the history that is put forward as the premise for current turns, it summons a past where the lines between scholar and author, or scientist and artist, are less distinct.

Defending sociology against accusations of 'vulgar scientism', Robert Nisbet explains that, in addition to canonical sociologists' commitment to the intricate literacy of social life, their methods were also a melange of scientific and poetic modes. 'Can anyone believe that Tönnies' typology of *Gemeinschaft* and *Gesellschaft*, Weber's vision of *rationalization*, Simmel's image of *metropolis*, and Durkheim's perspective of *anomie* came from logico-empirical analysis as it is understood today? Merely to ask the question,' Nisbet states, 'is to know the answer' (1966: 19). Nisbet argues that a scholar who claims that sociology stands squarely in a tradition of arid rationality misses the fact that '[e]ach [of these sociologists] was, with deep intuition, with profound imaginative grasp, reacting to the world around him, even as does the artist, and, also like the artist, objectifying internal and only partly conscious, states of mind' (19). Here the social scientist draws from intuition and hunches and imaginatively attempts to grasp the affective currents that emerge in a particular time and place. Sociology, in this longer history, however, is not firmly settled in the house of science, but has long been a provocateur of the two cultures' propriety.

Traversing the geographical terrain of France, Germany and Britain, Wolf Lepenies' *Between Literature and Science* (1988) offers a comprehensive retelling of sociology's *Bildungsroman* amid the 'two cultures'. Literature and sociology have, 'from the middle of the nineteenth century onward', according to Lepenies, 'contested with one another the claim to offer the key orientation for modern civilization and to constitute the guide to living appropriate to industrial society' (1988: 1). Along their fault lines several related conceptual oppositions are drawn, including reason and emotion, fact and fiction, evidence and experience, and reality and representation. As Johan Heilbron has written, in the early nineteenth century 'the idea that aesthetic activities ought to be completely separate from cognitive ones became more prevalent' and in this 'contest between science and literature, nothing and no one could avoid taking sides' (1995: 157). But where this conflict has endured it is also continually undermined. Lepenies suggests that the formative rift between sociology and literature came not from innate difference but from an uncomfortable overlap (13). 'In this competition over the claim to be the rule of life appropriate to industrial society,' Lepenies cautions, 'sociology cannot, however, simply be equated with rationality and literature with feeling' (13).

This account of sociology's coming-of-age proves useful for rethinking the structure of current methodological debates. Rather than a neat schism between the humanities and social sciences, we see a genealogy that spoils the supposed propriety of positivism versus poetry – novelists declaring themselves sociologists and sociologists heavily indebted to novelists. Lepenies cites many forbears that mix science and literature as knowledge, for instance Goethe's influence, as both natural scientist and poet, upon most scholars in the emerging modern European academy. As another example, the naturalist and cosmologist Comte de Buffon, whose 36-volume of natural history was 'read by every intellectual in Paris', influenced the novelist Honoré de Balzac, who in turn influenced Karl Marx and Friedrich Engels, and Marcel Proust (who was also indebted to French philosopher Henri Bergson (Bisson [1945] 1988: 3)). In England, sociology also has literature in its genetic mix: Comte's correspondent John Stuart Mill's utilitarian sociology was influenced by his dedicated study of romantic poetry (Davis 1985) and in Germany the novels of Thomas Mann stylised the ideas of his correspondent Max Weber for the literary public (Goldman 1988 and 1992).

Just as sociology drew from literature, novelists also claimed the mantle of sociology. According to Lepenies: 'When [Émile] Zola spoke of the "*sociologie pratique*" that characterised his novels he implied that in the last resort it was he who practised true sociology' (7). Lepenies also includes Charles Dickens as a social novelist *and* critic of social theory, explaining that *Hard Times* (1854) is a satire of 'the dehumanising effects of the utilitarianism of a James Mill', the founder, along with Jeremy Bentham, of utilitarianism (1988: 13;

see also Fielding 1956).[5] In later years, in England, the novelists' claim to produce social inquiry continued. In 1906, for instance, H. G. Wells gave a lecture to the Sociological Society at the London School of Economics titled 'The So-called Science of Sociology', dismissing the discipline's scientific status and pioneers, such as Auguste Comte (Wells 1914: 141–51). Elsewhere, Wells claimed that 'the modern novel [. . .] is the only medium through which we can discuss the great majority of the problems which are being raised in such bristling multitude by our contemporary social development' (Wells 1914: 121). Wells contended that literature had always done the work of sociology and that the introduction of a dedicated pseudo-science could not usurp the social novelist's practice. These tangled lineages, the interweaving of methods and interests and the chafing tension of overlap, unsettle the received history of poetic versus scientific methods.

Lepenies further complicates the divide between the arts and social sciences by tracing how the biographies and careers of the scholars that wage these arguments often contradict their polemical allegiances. As with the contemporary proposals I discuss in this book, method proposals of the nineteenth century were also based on autobiographical readings of the political climate. In Lepenies' 'secret history of the modern social sciences' (1988: 14) love, depression, rivalries, class factions, generational conflicts, resentment, jealousy or the struggle to maintain a career, leverage and undermine arguments that oppose reason and judiciousness to creativity and emotion. Lepenies offers us the history of the division between sociology and literature that Parkhurst Ferguson et al. would later describe as 'an antagonism, as durable as it is simplistic' (1988: 49). But he also gives us another history, a meta-history that contributes a sense of the contestation that reproduces this rift, but also challenges its sustainability. In this disciplinary chronicle, how truth and

---

[5] Dickens continues to be invoked as a social theorist; for instance, Gilles Deleuze and Félix Guattari use a passage from Dickens to illustrate his theory of immanence in 'Immanence: A Life' (1996). This use of literature to point to a place where an idea already operates is common in social theory. Freud draws on mythology and literature in much of his work, particularly in 'The Uncanny' ([1919] 2003). Similarly, Erving Goffman uses the work of Herman Melville in *Asylums* (1961).

knowledge operate, how they are lived by the very theoreticians involved in the debate, points to something beyond the propriety of discipline. The social scientist's attempt to separate evidence from experience, to enact positivism without personal perspective, or to detach from desire, always trips over itself. The literary critic's inverse efforts meet a similar fate.

This history locates a challenge to the division of emotion and reason at sociology's very formation. Auguste Comte, the founder of sociology ([1848] 1865), for instance, forsook his initially strict division of parable and positivism when appealing to the heart of the Catholic novelist Clotilde de Vaux (Pickering 1994). Via their letters to one another, we can trace a transformation of Comte's positivist science – originally anti-theological – into a positivist religion that 'united thoughts, feeling and action – with the goal of perfecting the outer and inner existence of man' (Lepenies 1988: 29). As Heilbron writes, Comte was initially disconnected from the artists and writers of the Paris salon scene – 'what he called "positive" was quite the opposite of "poetic"' (Heilbron 1995: 217). But later 'he discovered the power of emotion' and 'literature and music began to play a meaningful role in his life' (217). The influence of de Vaux upon Comte was a Parisian love story (sadly for Comte, unrequited) that marked 'a bizarre episode in the history of the social sciences' that 'later led Comte's successors to divide into two separate strands' (Lepenies 1988: 35). The sociologist in this founding tale recalibrates his science, driven in part by love and desire: his life work is a web of personal and professional stakes. From Comte's biography it is clear that the sociological method is not all measurement and rationality, neither does it ignore the phenomenological or emotional; it is also made up of experiences, desires and contingencies.

By sociologising the founding tracts of sociology, Lepenies reframes the question of disciplinary identity as the question of identity proper. While he focuses on the difficulties of a discipline trying to account for human nature, he gestures toward the possibility that what complicates the project is the fact that anyone who takes on this task is actually faced with the broader, and often subliminal, difficulty of trying to account for and sustain their social world. In doing this, Lepenies cleverly muddles the separateness of reason and passion, or the disparate logics that are assumed to mark sociology as literature's other. 'The conflict between cold reason and the culture of feeling, typical of the competition between the social sciences and literature', Lepenies states, 'is not confined to the realm of scientific and literary publications: it also sets its stamp on the lives, private and public, of the writers and scholars we are to consider' (1988: 14). Like Comte's positivism, a discipline is transformed as it is lived and used, and logic is influenced by the demands of the moment.

To think of method in this way problematises the assumption that one method can be straightforwardly hailed as the corrective, or untroubled successor, of another. If the method itself is *of* social life it becomes difficult to simply dismiss a method as if it were an external apparatus, outgrown by reality. What this context brings to the current debate is a sense that methods, and the judgments we make about them, are not things that happen separately from the social life we seek to study and document. The solution then cannot be to pursue a new and unsullied approach. How methods and judgements themselves come to be articulated must also be part of our thinking. For example, what is it that makes suspicion so dominant as the feeling of inquiry within a particular period? What produces scholars' faith in this wary orientation, and then a couple of decades later, an unforgiving distrust? Instead of seeing only some methods as affective, here the question is about how the affectivity of any and all methods is re/determined in their ongoing use and production, like a memory reconstructed with each act of remembering.

The 'Crisis of Representation': Ethnography Debates in the 1980s

As this return to sociology's origins demonstrates, interest in genres and their affects has not, up until now, been dormant in the academy. The post-critical interest in affect theory is only the latest iteration of a methodological question alive across centuries, cultures and fields, and more recent precedents feed into present concerns. Here again, looking back rather than forward, there are insights to be gained which unsettle the polemic drawn between affect and critique. As late as the 1980s we can find a precedent for debates about the politics of experimenting with methods in social science. Here I turn to these discussions, known as 'the ethnography debates', which sought to open up ethical questions about how anthropology could reform its methods in the wake of postcolonial critiques. This discussion is particularly insightful for current methodological proposals, because rather than advocating for some methods over others, it reckoned with the ethical and representational issues that are implicit in all attempts to analyse and document social life.

In *Blurred Genres: The Reconfiguration of Social Thought* (1980), Clifford Geertz explains that the act of playing with and testing generic rules has a long and diverse history. Writing well before the current turn, Geertz pinpointed the blurring of genres as a mounting trend but, importantly, not one that was restricted to certain styles or to importing the ideas of one field into the form of another. For him, it is not only critical methods that 'pin down', nor is it only creative genres that can ebb and flow along with life. In his typically opinionated manner, Geertz lists a mutability and manipulability across all genres:

> [P]hilosophical inquiries looking like literary criticism (think of Stanley Cavell on Beckett or Thoreau, Sartre on Flaubert), scientific discussions looking like belles lettres *morceaux* (Lewis Thomas, Loren Eiseley), baroque fantasies presented as deadpan empirical observations (Borges, Barthelme), histories that consist of equations and tables or law court testimony (Fogel and Engerman, Le Roi Ladurie), documentaries that read like true confessions (Mailer), parables posing as ethnographies (Castenada), theoretical treatises set out as travelogues (Lévi-Strauss), ideological arguments cast as historiographical inquiries (Edward Said), epistemological studies constructed like political tracts (Paul Feyerabend), methodological polemics got up as personal memoirs (James Watson). (Geertz 1980: 19)

By presenting genre experimentation as something ongoing rather than novel, Geertz lends a different historical context to the proposals I analyse in the following chapters of *Critical Affect*. As he notes, works from the nineteenth and twentieth centuries already acknowledge, indeed play with, the flexibility of authority not only of 'creative' genres, but the mercurial notion of disciplinary writing styles more generally. In some cases, the most recent iterations of the fact/fiction divide are *more* conservative, especially in the way they characterise, even caricature, genres as quite set. In contrast, far from seeing scholarly forms as dry and inert, literary provocateurs of the nineteenth century realised and took advantage of the authoritative affects of the equation, the table and the tract. Furthermore, Geertz suggests that social scientists have always utilised this 'intellectual poaching licence', explicitly aiming to do what every other genre already does implicitly: 'trying to discover order in collective life' (20). Thus, while social scientists may currently seek to reorient their work within alternative disciplinary genealogies (often back through Gilles Deleuze, in a fashion so cursory as to be criticised repeatedly even by those making these arguments[6]), a rich and challenging history for their intervention into the ethics of blurred genres is already present – and arguably most obvious – within social science.

This chapter illuminates a different way of viewing the trajectory of intellectual work: rather than seeing theoretical innovation as a linear path to progress, with each new crop of thinkers learning from and reforming the errors of the generation passed, we can see how the same issues turn up again and again, often changing form before they are resolved, and sometimes actually slinking back into more conservative or reductive iterations. While the manifestos of the broadly defined ontological turn claim to have moved away from poststructuralism's obsession with representation and its discontents, powerful resonances with past methodological interventions

---

[6] In *Non-Representational Theory*, Thrift criticises the blind faith of his peers' Deleuzianism. Thrift warns against what he describes as the 'spirit guide approach to social science', which he suggests is exemplified by the increasing popularity of a Deleuzian 'makeover' of people's work, 'that sometimes seems to resemble a religious conversion' (18). He states that he does not 'think that it is the function of a social scientist to simply apply the work of philosophers' (Thrift 2007: 18). In her work on affect and fictocriticism, Anna Gibbs is similarly critical of the often-tokenistic invocation of Deleuzian terminology. Gibbs argues that other possible precedents for fictocriticism are 'too often ignored in favour of simple citation of (as opposed to actual use of), for example, Deleuze' (2005: 3). She adds: 'Here I speak as a passionate reader of Deleuze, but one dismayed by his dismal impact especially on postgraduate work in Australia, as thought seems increasingly to be replaced by jargonistic replication' (9).

remain. For example, George E. Marcus and Michael M. J. Fischer's original definition of 'the crisis of representation' could easily double for a definition of the affective turn's *raison d'être*. However, the lineage is all wrong: in the ethnography debates the linguistic turn, poststructuralism and postcolonial theory are credited with ushering in greater recognition of how ethnography produces rather than merely documents culture. In *Anthropology as Cultural Critique: An Experimental Moment in the Human Sciences* (1986), they explain that:

> [The crisis of representation] is the intellectual stimulus for the contemporary vitality of experimental writing in anthropology. The crisis arises from uncertainty about adequate means of describing social reality. In the United States, it is an expression of the failure of post-World War II paradigms, or the unifying ideas of a remarkable number of fields, to account for conditions within American society, if not within Western societies globally, which seem to be in a state of profound transition. (8–9)

While a shift toward 'non-representational' methods aims to quell this crisis, the problem outlined, even its structure as an inherited issue that must be solved with a change in methods, resembles the current state of play.

The 'crisis of representation', as Marcus terms it, plays an undeniable, albeit under-acknowledged, role in grounding the current turn. There are striking parallels between the arguments made then and now, but also an interesting reluctance to explore the political relevance of this earlier work and its applicability to current dilemmas. The 1980s debates presented such enduring problems for the practice of ethnographic representation that Geertz acerbically described ethnography in their midst as 'a task at which no one ever does more than not utterly fail' (Geertz 1980: 143). Bruce M. Knauft captures the fatigue over the enduring crisis of representation when he surmises that '[t]he debates of the 1980s and early 1990s – concerning experimental ethnography and reflexivity, science and pseudo-science, objectivity versus evocation and the subject-position of the author – have lost their energy and their sense of either accomplishment or struggle' (Knauft 2006: 407). In light of these descriptions, it seems likely that the omission of this

legacy in more contemporary discussion is symptomatic of the legacy itself, specifically the irresolvable difficulties it poses for notions
of evidence and form. To begin with, situating present arguments
within this social science history rather than, for example, material-
ist philosophy, also highlights well-established reasons to be wary of
casting certain genres as more caring and protective (Latour 2004:
232) or truthful (Taussig, in Strauss, 2005: unpaginated) than others.
The ethical turmoil involved in trying to *authentically* represent the
truth of a particular person or community is not abated by a neat
schism between emotion and evidence, reality and representation
or ideology and practice, precisely because it is the instability of
how these categories are defined that lies at the heart of the crisis
of representation. The question is not about *which* genre, but about
genre itself – how does any mode of writing manipulate, albeit with
different tactics and effects.

It must be noted that the inclusive ambition of touchstone texts like
Marcus and James Clifford's edited volume *Writing Culture* (1986) was
undermined by a profound gender imbalance in its curated authorship (Hockey and Dawson 1997; Behar and Gordon 1995). Though
certainly flawed in that regard, *Writing Culture* opened important conversations about the ethics and politics of writing ethnography and
the potential to experiment as a critical practice.

The fact that fieldwork may result in a poem or a fragment, or
that it discusses affect instead of structure, does not change the essential reality that the social scientist is positioned as 'the one' to interpret and represent another person's life to wider publics. The term
'*crisis* of representation' is, for this reason, perhaps misleading. As
Lauren Berlant argues in a different context, 'the genre of crisis can
distort something structural and ongoing within ordinariness into
something that seems shocking and exceptional' (2011: 7). 'Crisis'
suggests a fraught moment, an exceptional period, the final impetus
before a resolution, but in fact what anthropology is left with is 'the
question of representation', the moniker of an unendingly fraught
political reality that is not resolved by rerouting the problem into a
question about genre choice.

It is perhaps because of this enduring representational 'crisis' that
social scientists are being drawn to calls to take up creative writing
or performance as modes of academic research. The latter sidestep

the deadlock of these issues when they advocate creative forms and dispersed authorship as more ethical methodologies. However, for contemporary social scientists to evade this history is to ignore an intervention which insisted on considering the pragmatic and lived effects summoned by *all* modes of representation and scholarship. Edward Said, after all, did not simply aim his criticisms at ethnography, as though different literary genres might escape the problem. According to Said: '*This* Orientalism can accommodate Aeschylus, say, and Victor Hugo, Dante and Karl Marx' (1978: 3). In other words, genres of both fiction and non-fiction were seen as equally capable of perpetuating colonial stereotypes and othering their subjects. To now divide genres into either creative or critical categories, supposedly in answer to the same question of method and ethics, seems a forgetful move.

Writing later in the decade, Marilyn Strathern, renowned for her feminist intervention into the discipline of anthropology, further highlights the point that shifting genre does not elide questions about the ethics of authorship. She states that 'whether a writer chooses (say) a "scientific" style or a "literary" one signals the kind of fiction it is; there cannot be a choice to eschew fiction altogether' (1987: 257). As Strathern suggests here, any genre is an act of authorial interpretation; all genres are fictions, in that they are all selectively manipulated and created. She explains that we 'typically think of anthropologists as creating devices by which to understand what other people think or believe. Simultaneously, of course, they are engaged in constructing devices by which to affect what their audience thinks and believes' (1987: 256). This practice does not change because the ethnographer writes poetry. Poetry is also a manipulative figural device. For this reason there is a certain regression in current calls to shift to creative genres as a way to escape the problems inherent in presenting evidence. It overlooks an insight that was already established by the previous ethnography debates, namely that *all* genres are implicated in the political and ethical actions of the times in which they are authored and the times in which they are read.

In the context of such historical precedents and their immediate complication of the critical/creative division, the rush to embrace a forward-looking, avant-garde fervour proves a problematic aspect of the celebratory turn to 'creative' methods as more neutral, sensitive or responsive. A presumption that creative engagements with affect are unadulterated and pure expressions, free of judgement and agenda – that they are somehow ethically superior – does little to encourage an engagement with the mess of truth-telling practices and the partiality with which genres are determined or recast. Seen in this light, this alternative genealogy gives us pause to reconsider the structure of current arguments and specifically the way they set up fixed identities and capacities for different methods that are either negative or positive, creative or critical, caring or iconoclastic, perfunctory or responsive.

Emotional Truth and the Ethics of 'the True Story': New Journalism and Memoir

In this final example of a genre debate, attention falls on the modes of reading that exist beyond the academy. In several of the methods proposals I have briefly outlined, such as Felski's, the assumption is that less critical approaches, which are described as aesthetic or emotional engagements, are more akin to how people respond to phenomena and how they make sense of their everyday attachments and relations. As I will discuss in more detail in Chapter 3, several proposals actively argue for scholars to write in poetic forms, or use film or performance, on the basis that such approaches are less fraught with the ethical and methodological issues of critique. In these proposals there is no evidence that people actually find creative methods more relatable or ethical. When we do look to public discourse around genres there are echoes of a 'two cultures' structure. But it is also clear that ethical issues are not associated with only some genres. Rather, conflicts are waged over the social process of genre determination more broadly. For example, in the fields of narrative journalism and auto/biography, readers and critics have debated how far writers can blur the lines of fact and fiction and yet still tell a *true* story. Public discussions arising around particular cases have scrutinised and tested what constitutes evidence and representational ethics. They dissect the very rules and capacities of truth-telling genres and reveal how such rules are constantly unfixed and refigured.

To provide an overview, again here truths tend to be divided into two types. In the terminology common to these debates, on the one side we have 'emotional truth' which fictional texts are thought to capture, and on the other side factual truth which is the expected foundation of non-fiction writing. 'Emotional truth' is often diffusely defined, though commonly it denotes 'a true story' that does not find its basis in the actual particulars of one case but offers a composite or representative story which resonates – or 'rings true' – with a collective of people. The claim of certain writers, as I will explain, is that veering from the facts can be necessary to get to a deeper truth of collective experience. Tension emerges when emotional truth becomes the basis of non-fiction, such as journalism or memoir, which is, even allowing for creativity and style, still widely presumed to be based in factual truth. Often social backlash has arisen around a 'hoax', when it is revealed that a text readers thought to be non-fiction contains elements of fiction. What becomes evident in these cases is that the capacity of genres is not fixed; rather the tropes of non-fiction can be used to *indicate* a factual basis and yet be entirely fabricated. What *is* seemingly fixed are people's expectations of the genre, but these are also, when held up to scrutiny, deeply contingent upon the social context.

This division roughly aligns with the idea of a critical, erudite mode of truth-telling that is based on modes of detection and fact-finding paired with an inclusive, fluid mode of truth-telling based on attunement and creative experimentation that we see in work on critique and affect. But at the same time there are key – and informative – differences. In debates around narrative journalism and memoir, we hear complex ethical discussions about how people read genres and how contingent the assumed structures of such genres are on the social context in which they are written and read. As examples from this field show, far from fixed, the capacities of different modes of truth-telling are made and remade in both their creation and consumption. At stake here is why the rules of genre are important to people. When there are claims that fictionalising or compositing aspects of people's lives is necessary to capture the 'emotional truth' of experience, a series of critical questions about the ethics of representation arise, including who can speak for the truth of a life and with whose permission? What specificities are lost in favour of the general and why might these details, and their selection, matter?

In some cases, readers are lenient with the rules of genre and how a life may be represented and verified. The blurring of fact and fiction may be warranted if a profile or biography achieves its audience's desire to be viscerally close to its subject and present in its myth-affirming world. But this is not always so. The methods by which society authenticates life-narratives, like lives themselves, are 'not all of one piece' and do not 'lend [themselves] to one interpretation exclusively' (Guralnick 1995: xiii). Genres, and the authorial responsibilities people ascribe to them, are at turns mercurial and rigid in public culture, shaping the way stories can be read and told. Authorship, in this sense, is a social process where it is no longer clear why or with whom a narrative specifically and straightforwardly originates. Where this authorial practice becomes most provocative, however, is in the social desire to determine such a source nonetheless. The question that emerges from this unsteady, yet determined, social process is one of accountability in terms of what is responsible *and* what is tellable, rather than a question about which genre is most caring. It is a query that applies to all genres: from where is the authority to tell a particular story derived and how is its veracity constituted?

To consider an example, after being endorsed by Oprah Winfrey as a 'brave, survivor narrative', James Frey's best-selling memoir *A Million Little Pieces* (2006) was infamously revealed to have fabricated the felonies Frey claimed to have committed and the time in prison he alleged he had served for them. In response to the media's accusations of fraud, Frey claimed that people derive different kinds of truths from life-stories, that the authenticity and power of the story need not be verifiable or based strictly on factual accounts. Frey defended the liberties he'd taken with the claim that his story still had an 'emotional truth' (CNN Transcript 2006) or lent an affective authenticity to an exemplary event. In a public defence of Frey's book, Winfrey also affirmed the value of this kind of truth, claiming:

> The underlying message of redemption in James Frey's novel still resonates with me ... whether or not the car's wheels rolled up

on the sidewalk or whether he hit the police officer or didn't hit
the police officer is irrelevant to me. What is relevant is that he
was a drug addict who spent years in turmoil . . . [he] stepped out
of that history to be the man that he is today, and to take that
message to save other people and allow them to save themselves.
(Winfrey, in CNN Transcript 2006)

Frey argued that the liberties he took with the actual events were
for the sake of communicating the 'essential truth' of a life of drug
and alcohol addiction. Because the emotional impact is the primary goal, Frey's elaborations are apparently justified. In the above
excerpt, Winfrey affirms this, placing the truth-value on the *efficacy*
of the memoir rather than its veracity.

However, in an act that emphasises the social *and* personal contingency of such evaluations, Winfrey later withdrew her support for
Frey in response to public pressure, and broadcast an apology for her
'mistake' (Dahmen 2010: 124). In a *New York Times* editorial, Winfrey
was praised for this action: 'Ms. Winfrey gave the audience . . . what it
was hoping for: a demand to hear the truth' (cited in Dahmen 2010:
124). Winfrey's equivocation about what should constitute 'the truth'
demonstrates the power of what Nancy K. Miller terms 'common
cultural consensus' (2007: 541). Winfrey was allowed to change her
position, indeed she was praised for this, only because she eventu-
ally made what was popularly verified to be the 'right' choice. Her
attribution of emotional truth to a non-fiction genre, to a genre that
most readers assume to be factual, was quickly downplayed.

Hoaxes disrupt the safety of genre and push us to scrutinise how
we routinely read. A group of Frey's readers filed a federal class-
action lawsuit claiming that, due to such a genre betrayal, reading
the book had been a waste of time for which they should be reim-
bursed financially (Dahmen 2010: 116). They were offended because
they felt changed by his memoir, its testimony to addiction had
informed their lives but then they were forced to question how this
could happen if the story was not true. In this case, emotional truth
seems to require permission from the audience in which it evokes
resonance. The mode that is considered more creative and affective
is not automatically more intuitive or ethical, or more true to life,
but rather has its own shifting set of ethical codes and parameters

which are determined not only by its authors. This is the kind of complexity of reception that makes the wholesale promotion of creative genres over critical genres unsound.

In 'False Documents' (1977), E. L. Doctorow attempts to locate emotional truth historically, suggesting that 'it is possible there was a time in which the designative and evocative functions of language were one and the same" (217). Drawing on Walter Benjamin's 'The Storyteller' (1968), Doctorow notes that fiction was once looked to for life counsel: 'If the story was good the counsel was valuable and therefore the story was true' (218–19). In this assertion, the story is attributed a truth based on its affectiveness, on its ability to 'move' its audience. The notion of truth rattled the field of journalism in the 1970s and 1980s, when Joseph Mitchell, an acclaimed journalist at *The New Yorker*, insisted that he wanted his 'stories to be truthful, rather than factual' (Mitchell 1992: 373). Despite attracting criticism, similar statements recur in the words of more contemporary non-fiction writers. Vietnam Veteran writer Tim O'Brien has also defended the use of a shared, emotional literacy as a form of verification in autobiographical fiction. Explaining his blurring of fact and fiction, O'Brien argued that 'a story's truth shouldn't be measured by happening but by an entirely different standard, a standard of emotion, feeling – "does it ring true?" as opposed to "is it true?"' (Naparsteck and O'Brien 1991: 10). As I will discuss at length in Chapter 3, there are also academic instances, including anthropologist Michael Taussig, who argued that 'fiction allowed me to be more truthful' (Strauss 2005: unpaginated) in writing his ethnography, *The Magic of the State* (1997). These claims that one can be more truthful by being less factual are provocative, not only because they ask us to rethink notions of veracity, but because they challenge the usual alliance of emotional truth with fiction and factual truth with non-fiction.

Evidence of the association of emotional truth with fiction is illustrated in Robert S. Boynton's interview with narrative journalist Richard Preston (Boynton 2005). The discussion centred on the narrative style of New Journalism, which caused public anxiety over the mixing of verifiable and emotional truth genres, specifically the use of fictive devices such as 'interior character development', in reporting (Wolfe 1975, cf. Markel 1972 and Otzick 1973). When asked whether the literary forms of New Journalism could capture truth, Preston defined what he termed 'emotional and cultural truth' (Boynton 2005: 321). Preston explains that emotional and cultural truth is 'the truth that one encounters in [Henry] Fielding's preface to Tom Jones, in which he argues that even though Tom Jones never really existed, his story is "true" because it tells the human truth. It is the true depiction of the human condition and human emotions' (321). This is the truth that is assigned to fiction, in which characters are not considered real but their stories are thought to capture a profound collective truth. For Preston, the fictional tropes of New Journalism make it capable of this kind of truth, but not the verifiable truth of traditional journalism.

Preston's definition describes an emotional truth as a fable, not to be taken literally. He assumes that readers know this and read with caution. However this definition does not necessarily capture the fluidity of how truth is negotiated. We draw across tenuous and counterintuitive sources to collate and verify our account of the world, constantly confounding received notions of which words and representations have weight. As such, people may read stories verified by emotional truths as proscriptive. Several cases could be investigated further to highlight this fact. In journalist Jon Krakauer's *Into the Wild* (1996), Christopher McCandless, a young, runaway hiker, dies from poisoning and starvation in close range of several stocked rangers' cabins because his map of Alaska derives from Jack London stories rather than the parks' authority (173). Another case could be Johann Wolfgang von Goethe's *The Sorrows of Young Werther* [1774] (2006), which inspired young men to commit suicide, or Orson Welles' infamous radio adaptation of H. G. Wells' *War of the Worlds* (1938), which caused public hysteria with its seemingly real depiction of alien invasion. In short, people may not always recognise, or indeed *want* to recognise, the nuanced markers of genre, but are affected in productive ways nevertheless.

In questioning the alliance of truth-value with genre it is important not to overlook how powerful such divisions are, even when porous. Doctorow, perhaps motioning to the realising power of all genres, proclaims that there 'is no longer any such things as fiction or non-fiction; there's only narrative' (1977: 219). However, while it is fair to say that the sovereignty of these categories is enduringly under question, as the reaction to the Frey controversy illustrates, people do perceive fiction and non-fiction as distinct genres that make different demands upon readers' engagement. It is the genre, not simply the story, which indicates the level of emotional investment and empathy a reader will devote. A life story is socially evaluated, but so is its method of delivery. False documents or identity hoaxes do not wholly collapse the distinctions we make between fact and fiction, between emotional and verifiable truths, or between experience and evidence. Indeed, in many cases they actually reify them, and yet they illuminate, nevertheless, what is at stake in these, shifting, distinctions.

Social debates about authorship and authenticity challenge us to reconsider how we routinely read lives and stories as conforming to pre-existing forms with clearly delineated purposes and responsibilities. When the rules of genre are broken we realise the complexity with which they are upheld. Forced to be reflexive, people are faced with the challenge of the biographer: 'The moment one begins to investigate the truth of the simplest facts which one has accepted as true it is as though one has stepped off a firm narrow path into a bog or a quicksand' (Woolf, in Guralnick 1994: xii). By teasing out the various positions, paradoxes and conflicts within public conjecture about the ethics of representation we are faced with the dynamic intricacy of seemingly prosaic, and intrinsic, laws. How people read or verify testimony, for instance, is and is not governed by the set rules of fixed genres. Literature may be read as an emotionally true fable, but it might also be read as an instructive guide about how best to live, or as a historical and factual account of real-life events. Consciously or unconsciously it may also be read as a mix of all of these things. Such a complex picture troubles the shift to creative genres as a mode that is presumably less critical and more ethical for social scholarship. Issues with how we account for life not only apply to all genres but question the very acts by which we determine the rules, feelings and identities of different forms. Critical and affective considerations here are intimately interlinked.

Opening the Question of Method

While the current turn against critique presents the adoption of new methods as a natural next step, put in the context of existing conversations about genre and ethics, questions remain about how the authenticity of representational modes is being adjudicated. By opening up these past cases, this chapter reframes recent methodological directives not as a new slate, but as the continuation of enduring conflicts about discipline, methodology, ethics and the nature of veracity. This history foregrounds a genealogy that is less neat and thus lends itself less easily to a revolution in method. The turn against critique sets up a problem where past methods – specifically what are seen to be critical and suspicious modes of reading and analysis – are outgrown and stand in the way of discovering more relevant and careful approaches. The structure of this argument assumes a 'two cultures' form, where critique is cast as rote and authoritative and new methods are cast as nimble and receptive.

Given this, the current negotiations with disciplinary propriety offer a rich ground to rethink what is at stake in a more enduring intellectual opposition between what are seen to be either creative *or* critical attempts to document social life. The question then shifts from *which* method is troublesome or promising, to be about the very structure of methodological debates: why does this oppositional structure recur and what is at stake in it? As the constant refiguring of a two cultures conflict shows, this underlying query cannot be answered by proving one method of interpretation to be superior to another. The texture and fate of the two cultures is determined in the way it is negotiated. Attention to this level of the methodological quests I examine is vital if we are to address the counterintuitive ways that certain lives and narratives come to be fixed with meaning and validity. If we can begin to include the pursuit of method as part of this process of accountability, rather than just the better or worse means to access it, we could consider how social forms of narration, including social science, might already confound the long-standing division of the literary and the social *and* its correlative hierarchies of truth-value.

This first chapter raises questions that inform those to follow: what is at stake in accepting the thinly drawn portraits of critique and its antidotes? Do we get closer to a humble and more accurate mode of social explanation; or alleviate long-running issues around ethics and representation; or begin to build a more inclusive and generous form of social inquiry? Here I have also contextualised the following chapters' analysis of key arguments against critique that deal directly with the division of emotional and verifiable truths. I examine these methodological directives as cases with which to rethink the divisions that are routinely drawn, though in fascinatingly paradoxical ways, between verifiable facts and lived interpretations.

Method, read this way, is an expression of the nebulous social it seeks to document, rather than an error or an antidote. Unfixed, the identity and capacities of a method are akin to what sociologist Avery F. Gordon defines as the identity of a person or 'complex personhood'. This way of thinking about how we read the world unsteadies a polemic hierarchy of genres and presumptions about their fixed and predictable abilities to engage with truth and experience. The person is actual, they are anchored and workably coherent, but they also 'remember and forget, are beset by contradiction, and recognize and misrecognise themselves and others' (2008: 4). For Gordon, 'complex personhood means that the stories people tell about themselves, about their troubles, about their social worlds and about their society's problems are entangled, and weave between what is immediately available as a story and what their imaginations are reaching towards' (4). What is documented as evidence then, even in the case of statistics or census results, are facts that are reported from a reservoir of reason and emotion, of actuality and aspiration, pre-existing narratives and stabs in the dark. The fact itself is a jumble of these things; the process by which it is collected and reported is another layer again. Knowledge works as a solid force of verification but it is also in flux. What is socially accepted as true at one point in history is discarded, or derided, at another. The history of intelligence, nutrition, the canonisation of saints and countless other bodies of knowledge are constantly being rearranged and reconstituted as facts and the ways we measure them change.

The reason that it is difficult to account for the complexity of social decisions is not because we do not yet have the right method, but because method itself *is* this process of complex decision-making. The rush to 'the new' risks overlooking the ways that existing methods, perhaps even in their brittleness and difficulty, are already live and multivalent expressions that refigure an always dynamic intellectual heritage. By working closely with key arguments from the turn against critique in the following chapters I explore how we might *stay with* what appears to be an error, impasse or recuperation in theoretical arguments as the very place to open up and investigate their emotional and methodological complexity. What are the shapes of these judgements, what is the nature of their evidence and what are the hopes of their aims? By attending closely to these arguments, we can see how a division between affect and critique operates but is also often undermined by the productive entanglement of critical affects – where feelings of suspicion and concerns about authorship remain a key part of our affective response to socio-political currents.

2

Evidence in Flux

Emotional and verifiable truths are not strictly separate in social life. However, the assumed division of labour between the social sciences and the humanities, the idea that one deals with real life and the other only with the representations of that life, makes recognising this crossover challenging. As detailed in the previous chapter, several recent proposals have attempted to address this disjuncture. Though far from alleviating political contestation around what forms of truth-telling will be accepted, these academic efforts are equally fraught with questions about whether a truth should be verifiable or emotionally resonant, whether a story is best told through critical or creative genres and who has the right to decide how the boundaries between these forms will be drawn.

The 'critique of critique' is one such proposal. Like 'surface reading,' this movement positions itself as an answer to the 'recent calls for alternatives to critical hermeneutics' and the perceived need to 'suspend routine [. . .] habits of paranoia and suspicion' (Love 2010: 387). Setting affect theory as the antidote to critical analysis, pitting ontology against epistemology and lived experience against bookish knowledge, the critique of critique settles squarely within both old and new debates about truth and genre. However, as this chapter will illustrate, rather than challenging the terms by which this debate has been waged, the hierarchy drawn between critical and 'new' methods maintains a division between emotional or verifiable truths, or facts and values. In the turn from critique, facts are still divided into those that are felt and those that are foundational. The reproduction of this structure troubles scholars' efforts to engage with the complexities of how people account for and verify their lives, often in ways that do not conform to such a binary.

To consider how we might keep the question of evidence open while also acknowledging the challenges of method's social context, this chapter traces two proposals frequently cited as influential for the turn from critique toward affect theory and/or alternative methods. These are Bruno Latour's 'Why Has Critique Run Out of Steam? From Matters of Fact to Matters of Concern' (2004) and Eve Kosofsky Sedgwick's 'You're So Paranoid You Probably Think This Introduction is About You: Paranoid Reading and Reparative Reading' (1997). Aside from being highly influential, the arguments of Latour and Sedgwick are of interest because, for them, the turn is not only an imperative for scholarship generally, but also for shifts in their own intellectual and political interests. On the surface, these arguments affirm a polemic around the question of genre: critique is static and predictable, whereas 'composition', to use Latour's term, can express the fluidity of life. However, if we look more closely at their living formulation, in the tradition of Wolf Lepenies (1988), these proposals are themselves evidence of the dynamic terms by which veracity is negotiated.

Thus drawing out the formulation of the turn against critique, the following investigation demonstrates how two of its key proponents' own critical turning points are verified by a dynamic evidentiary process that enlists personal convictions, political investments, critical concerns and sneaking suspicions. Though they rationalise the forms of evidence certain genres can use and the truths they can produce, within these arguments themselves genres of evidence are porous. The opposition between felt and verified knowledge, or experience and facts, is averred but not sustained. Mercurial in nature, these scholars' methods of verification unsettle their premise that critical and affective engagements are essentially opposed.

Opening up these paradoxes, this chapter locates unresolved questions – about how and why genre structures and their truth-values are produced – at the root of the critique of critique's methodological corrective. Unpacking this paradox is particularly important because although Sedgwick and Latour sideline the hermeneutics of suspicion, their work similarly struggles to put together an explanatory story by relating and conflating different, and often disparate, forms of proof. Though these arguments identify methods as fixed and essentially different – in both means and ends – they can also be seen to enact these same methods' contingent and lived complexities, thereby re-enlisting questions about how we determine the identity, value and capacities of critical methods.

Critical Conversions

Close attention to Latour's and Sedgwick's arguments reveals the enigmatic process by which particular notions about genres and their affects are verified. The most provocative entry point into this inquiry centres on the fascinatingly circular recuperation of paranoia as a dominant theme, and a position of defence, in arguments against the hermeneutics of suspicion. Creating a fundamental tension, suspicion operates as both the foil and motor of Latour's and Sedgwick's proposals. They dismiss paranoia through narratives that are hyper-paranoid and peppered with defensive metaphors of militarised, biological or cultural warfare.

It is important to note that for Sedgwick and Latour critique is a specific set of methods established during their own careers, including deconstruction and new historicism – methods of rereading that were often used to explore and challenge the implicit reproduction of political norms in canonical texts. The definition of 'critique' here does not follow the genealogy that Judith Butler, for instance, traces via Michel Foucault's 'What Is Critique?' ([1978] 2002) back to Immanuel Kant who advocated critique as a method for intellectual scrutiny, freedom and rigour (Butler 2002). However, the perception of critique is not unrelated to the specifically political context Butler outlines. Butler explains that, '[a]lthough critique clearly attains its modern formulation with philosophy, it also makes claims that exceed the particular disciplinary domain of the philosophical' (2002: 775). 'In Kant, for instance,' Butler notes, 'critique operates not only outside of philosophy and in the university more generally but also as a way of calling into question the legitimating grounds of various public and governmental agencies' (775). Here Butler contextualises critique as a form of pragmatic, political intervention. In the arguments discussed in this chapter, we are introduced to this form of critique as a faded enterprise. Though initially exponents of critical methods, Sedgwick and Latour both testify to their own living realisation of these methods' failure to 'call into question' social injustice or, rather, their failure to achieve anything beyond such a call.

Defining critique is therefore not just historical, but also autobiographical for the theorists discussed; the socio-historical setting for their arguments is their own experience of a paranoid zeitgeist. Latour's and Sedgwick's arguments against critique were published seven years apart and therefore in response to slightly different social determinants and events. Sedgwick's intellectual position develops amid the anxiety of the AIDS crisis, while Latour's is shaken by the political unrest over climate change and counter-terrorism. Furthermore, though Sedgwick's introduction appeared earlier than Latour's article, he does not cite it as a precedent. The two arguments cannot be presented as a direct genealogy though they express related concerns and are routinely cited together in critiques of critique.

Periods of political vulnerability for intellectuals – including the Cold War, the 1990s culture wars and more recent public debates about 9/11 and climate change – serve as the terms of reference in these method proposals. Latour's (2004) argument opens with the context of the cultural wars, the science wars and the War on Terror: events that sparked public debate around the contested nature and value of facts, beliefs and rhetoric (225). His critique of critique therefore intervenes into a field where the identity of facts is already open for discussion, a candour for which his earlier work argued. But it is a forum that, Latour suggests, now blurs the distinction between empirical scrutiny and flippant relativism, or deconstruction and conspiracy theory, and loses sight of how to gauge what is 'real'. Latour's article began as the Stanford Presidential Lecture in 2003 and his cultural references are predominantly American: the political strategy behind the invasion of Iraq; the Defense Advanced Research Projects Agency's appropriation of Baconian reason for its military slogan; the Alan Sokal/Social Text hoax; public conjecture about the cause of 9/11 (which also occurs in Latour's own French village); and the bizarre metaphors of George W. Bush's political speeches. Latour expresses his concern that, in this environment, scholars' continued use of critique – a method he sees as set to unmask cherished beliefs – only adds to the 'ruins' and 'destruction' of such conflicts (225). To further hone this image of counter-production, Latour presents critical methods as outdated and ill-equipped to match the rapid revision and mimicry of the political right. A fear that the humanities are losing ground in our increasingly corporate universities also simmers up in Latour's account of the intellectual climate. His stated concern is that critique, ostensibly seen as a crotchety and harsh method by 'fellow citizens', could be a contributing cause (239).

Sedgwick, writing seven years prior and less embroiled in the science wars, also describes the hermeneutics of suspicion as a method that chases its own tail and cannot register the mutable plurality of contemporary life. As I will explain, her perception is that we have lived through times that demanded a wary mindset – the witch-hunts of the Cold War, the Watergate Scandal and government fear-mongering over HIV and AIDS – but now face a new social atmosphere that requires less suspicious modes of reading. In the context of their own ideological shifts, these theorists argue that critique, a defence which was once essential to (their very own) political survival, has now become a mere defence mechanism, a perfunctory reflex. 'Are we [scholars] not', Latour (2004) asks, 'like those mechanical toys that endlessly make the same gesture when everything else has changed around them?' (225). For Sedgwick the political climate has changed; vigilance is no longer necessary or useful. For Latour, the defence – seized by conservative pundits – has become too predictable.

Basing their call for a disciplinary shift upon autobiographical turning points – experiential responses to political shifts – both proposals can be read as what Gerald Peters calls 'conversion narratives' (Peters 1993). To give context for this narrative archetype, Peters casts back to A. D. Nock's classic study of Christian conversion, which stated that religious conversions involve a reorientation of the soul of an individual, his deliberate turning from [. . .] an earlier form of piety, a turning which involves a consciousness that a great change is involved, that the old was wrong and the new is right (Nock 1933: 7). As Nock suggests, this 'reorientation' often forms a moral polemic, a sharp turn from 'wrong' to 'right'. We witness this conversion in Latour's and Sedgwick's manifestos as they denounce their former faith in critique and endorse new methodologies. This conversion is then set as a precedent for other scholars. However, when read closely, their narratives of conversion can be seen to bolster and defy the polemic differentiation of methods, as well as unsettle their simplified definitions of critique. The following sections unpack this verifying logic in firstly Latour's and then Sedgwick's arguments.

The 'Matter of Fact' as a 'Matter of Concern'

In the call for new methods, a provocative inconsistency arises between the general desire to be inclusive and an intolerance for scholarship that rests on suspicion. In Latour's argument this paradox generates a train of logic that cannot quite settle upon the source and boundaries of suspicious reasoning. At its first turn, for instance, critique is paranoid and imposes its negative schema upon social life. Latour argues that critical theory perfunctorily responds to everyday ideologies, facts and values with extreme paranoia and iconoclasm, and is thus no longer socially useful. The method, in his summation, is exhausted or, worse, has been co-opted into an ominous 'right wing'. Following this, Latour argues, critique cannot serve the real stuff of social life because it has become obsessed with the revelation of ideology and falsehood. In the wake of deconstruction, he explains, critics are geared to proving that myriad conspiracies of power underlie the prosaic relations of everyday life. According to Latour, they no longer trust or value facts in-themselves. Insisting that critical theory is infected with paranoia and bypasses the common candour of living, Latour advises scholars to elide critique.

However, in a curious turn, Latour also maintains that critical theory became paranoid because it was polluted by social methods of theorising, such as conspiracy theory. Lost from the academy's grip, a dumbed-down distortion of critique, used to question the validity of *all* scientific research and serve moral and political purposes, feeds back from the civic to spoil critical theory with its paranoid logic, its pathological distrust of facts. The public then, in Latour's plot, is first the victim of paranoid critique, and then its genesis. Thus, in arguing against critique, Latour insists we need to save facts from *and* for the very same 'everyday believers'. By this account, critique is both out of and too in-touch with the everyday attachments that fuel the culture wars, especially the selective verification of facts according to certain values.

With this contagion of knowledge occurring in the post 9/11 political landscape Latour describes, and within the logic of his very argument, Latour's seemingly uncomplicated shift in method is troubled. If both scholarly and social forms of discourse are riddled with paranoia, for example, can we so easily distinguish between the infection and the antidote? By Latour's own assessment, right-wing pundits ventriloquise left-wing critics and ivy league-educated intellectuals echo the rhetoric of common conspiracy theorists. In this greenhouse environment, Latour struggles with the task of determining propriety, such as where calls for revelation and exposure truly originate. This confusion generates an important series of overarching questions. For instance, does the dispersed agency of this social scene, the decentred form of agency Latour encourages, truly warrant the dismissal of a suspicious, critical reading? Or, does the symbiotic flare-up of suspicion in social *and* scholarly forums – and its impact on the viability of critique – suggest a more entangled notion of reality and methods of representation? Is Latour's own argument, for example, so different from the wary, critical arguments he suggests are no longer productive, albeit taking aim at the sociologist? What verifies Latour's own selection of which modes of truth-telling have value?

We can follow the tangled logic of determining the source and threat of paranoia in Latour's influential essay about the current state of critical inquiry, 'Why Has Critique Run Out of Steam? From Matters of Fact to Matters of Concern' (2004). To begin, Latour laments that the conspiracy theories of suspicious citizens have infected academic discourse. This is the turning point of Latour's narrative. His moment of conversion comes when he discerns a blur between left-wing and right-wing rhetoric – especially the charge that truths are being constructed in the name of values. He exemplifies this with what he suggests are the 'regrettable remarks' of Jean Baudrillard on 9/11. Baudrillard's analysis seeks to give credence to the power of the symbolic; Latour, however, is averse to this position. He asks: 'What has become of critique when a French general, no, a marshal of critique, namely, Jean Baudrillard, claims in a published book that the Twin Towers destroyed themselves under their own weight, so to speak, undermined by the utter nihilism inherent in capitalism itself [. . .]?' (Latour 2004: 228). Latour does not take up the point Baudrillard is trying to make but rather focuses on its alarming resonance with the words of a French villager who, in the same time period, scoffed at Latour's belief that terrorists rather than the CIA were responsible for the attack on the World Trade Center (228).

Though Baudrillard is not flippant about the events of 9/11 in the way this infers (Baudrillard 2003: 11–12), Latour is alarmed by what he hears as echoes of conspiracy theory in Baudrillard's and other thinkers' work. 'What's the real difference', he asks, 'between conspiracists and a popularised, that is teachable version of social critique inspired by a too quick reading of, let's say, a sociologist as eminent as Pierre Bourdieu?' (Latour 2004: 228–9). Latour finds 'something troublingly similar in the structure of the explanation, in the first movement of disbelief and, then, in the wheeling of causal explanations coming out of the deep dark below' (229). The concern here is clearly not with the rupture between social and sociological forms of inquiry but with their alarming similarity and the resultant difficulty in maintaining a hierarchy of truth-claims. Latour (2004) frames conspiracy theory, the social forums' improper adoption of 'critical thinking', as a home-grown antagonist:

> [C]onspiracy theories are an absurd deformation of our own arguments, but, like weapons smuggled through a fuzzy border to the wrong party, these are our weapons nonetheless. In spite of all the deformations, it is easy to recognize, still burnt in the steel, our trademark: Made in Criticalland. (230)

With this contamination metaphor Latour represents critique – a set-in-steel method – as spoiled. It has turned against the scholars who made it and taken over the critical enterprise. Critical reading, as it occurs in the public forum, is seen to be cheapened or commercialised, a deformed syndication, '[m]ade in Criticalland', of what Latour deemed to be proper critical theory in its elite, distillate form.

It is important to pause and note that Latour's argument at this point sounds like an argument against anti-intellectualism, akin to Louis Menand's 'Dangers Within and Without' (2005). Latour frames Baudrillard's foray into television as a compromise of scholarly rigour and Menand too is concerned by the tendency of academics to adopt the rhetoric of the public sphere in an attempt to be 'accessible'. Menand challenges this trend:

> The last premise academic humanists should be accepting is that the value of their views is measured by the correspondence of those views to common sense and the common culture. Being an intellectual and thinking theoretically *are* going outside the parameters of a common culture and common sense – whether it's string theory or deconstruction. What Derrida believed about how language works is not what the average newspaper reporter believes about how language works. Why is that a scandal? What are philosophers for? For that matter, what are universities for? It cannot be that universities exist to flatter the world's self-image. That work of flattery is being carried on by powers a million times greater than ours all the time. (16)

Like Latour, Menand is suspicious of the shared motifs in right-wing politics and academic discourse. However, whereas Menand concludes that: 'We are living in a country in which liberals would rather move to the right than offend the superstitions of the uneducated', and 'that this is an invitation we should decline without regrets' (17), Latour's argument takes a more enigmatic turn.

Despite his anxiety about conspiracy-contaminated critique, Latour cites the need to engage more generously with the beliefs, fetishes or common sense of everyday people as the motivation for a turn from critique. While it initially appears that Latour dislikes the infection across academic and quotidian discourses of belief, he then calls for the scholar not to dismiss the values of everyday believers, but to repair the ruins that are left in the wake of their own iconoclasm. Latour asserts that critique's limited narratives always give the critic the upper hand in unveiling the illusory fetishes of the 'naïve believer' (Latour 2004: 238) and have 'had the immense drawback of creating a massive gap between what was felt and what was real' (Latour 2010: 4).

Setting out his description of critique, Latour argues that '90 percent of the contemporary critical scene' can be summarised as using only two dismissive narrative schemas to discuss social life, both of which frame the everyday citizen, or 'naïve believer', as a fool and the critic as correct. The first is 'antifetishism', which Latour calls the 'fairy position'. He explains that, in this perspective: 'the courageous critic, who alone remains aware and attentive, who never sleeps, turns [the 'naive believers'] false objects into fetishes that are supposed to be nothing but mere empty white screens on which is projected the power of society, domination, whatever' (2004: 238). Latour diagnoses the second narrative, 'the fact position', as equally dismissive. He suggests that: 'this time it is the poor bloke, again taken aback, whose behaviour is now "explained" by the powerful effects of indisputable matters of fact: "You, ordinary fetishists, believe you are free but, in reality, you are acted on by forces you are not conscious of. Look at them, look, you blind idiot"' (242). These methods, which apparently encompass most of the critical work of the past century, are caricatured and set aside, though without specific, cited evidence. Latour offers this reductive characterisation of critical reading and yet his own critique is not a simple revelation of fact, an argument that fanatically pursues proof, but a testament to conviction, to a sense of reality and to experience. Thus Latour's critique is not simply one thing or another; it does not choose facts over values. It is polemic, acerbic and reductive at the very same time that it genuinely attempts to reassess our aims and actions, and to affect change.

Despite the quixotic nature of his own use of the critical genre, Latour's offers a clear-cut account of methods and their distinctly moral capacities. From 'matters of fact', he proposes a shift to 'matters of concern', where the question would not be whether a fact was true, but of what it was capable. To capture 'matters of concern' Latour offers 'composition' (2010) as the corrective of the corrective. 'My question is thus', he states: 'can we devise another powerful descriptive tool that deals this time with matters of concern and whose import then will no longer be to debunk but to protect and to care [...]?' (2004: 232). However, it is worth asking if the moral nature of both debunking and caring are more complex than this juxtaposition infers. This correction seems to assume that critical sociology operates solely to sleuth out illusions, rather than to highlight their productiveness and rethink how society might actualise alternative structures. Indeed, is the turn against critique itself not a form of ideology critique – concerned that scholars are unwittingly recuperating ingrained narratives, coerced by pressures to be 'knowing'? Moreover, the turn is methodological and aims to take common thought and motives seriously. But, in this conversion, everyday motives become strangely flat and benign. We might ask if the believer is always so naive or if their attachments always require the scholar's care and suspension of criticism?

In sum, what people believe and why they believe it may require something more than reparation and protection if we are to genuinely understand how conviction enacts political reality. While Latour speaks against Baudrillard to begin his argument, the semiotic approach of his fellow 'French general' complicates the agency of everyday beliefs. Baudrillard underlines the realising power of symbols and explores how the concrete is experienced on a day-to-day level, as a morally and existentially contested fact. In his account of 9/11, the Twin Towers are targeted for their symbolic potential in an act that is actually and symbolically destructive. The terrorism on 9/11 constitutes an act of war, as Baudrillard explains, not just because it destroyed buildings and lives, but also because it ruptured the cohesive narrative that holds a national, social, political and economic system together. The attack upon lower Manhattan was mobilised by the everyday faith in and animation of the act of terror's symbolic and affective potential, its value as a 'wounding punctum' in a narrative of political aggression (Barthes 1980). Engaging genuinely with attachments cannot be divorced from analysis of their connective social structures and the complex intermeshings of fantasy and reality that produce them. To open up analysis to recognise the agency of things, associations, networks and so on, as Latour does, need not come at the sake of analysing the material workings of law, culture and other collective forces, as if they are of two separate spheres or logics.

The dialogue between critical and common concerns that Latour asks for is already apparent, but in a form that warrants scepticism as much as generosity. What is a matter of fact and how facts are produced or maintained is a matter of concern for scholars and 'naïve believers'. The fact that people may not accept certain facts, or even disregard them in favour of a story with emotional resonance thus questioning what evidence holds value, does not mean that to those same people facticity is not important. The complexity of our engagement with the question of truth is that in some cases facts may be of the utmost salience to us and at other times have no real purchase. Latour's career exemplifies this variability. He questions scientific facts – indeed his early work inspired a widespread re-evaluation of how science's truths are produced (Latour and Woolgar 1979) – until that fact is one he believes in, such as climate change or the real threat of terror. The 'danger', according to Latour, comes not from 'an excessive confidence in ideological arguments posturing as matters of fact [. . .] but from an excessive distrust of good matters of fact disguised as bad ideological biases!' (227). To counter critique, Latour calls for 'a realist attitude' (245). But the underlying impetus of critique remains valid with continuing questions, as Latour's very argument proves, about who has the right to adjudicate which matters of fact are 'good' and which realities are 'real'. Latour's call to attention, in this vein, must surely also include careful analysis of why scholars feel drawn to methods of critique, or see an enduring value in mapping the structural determinants of individual choices, beliefs and actions – or the ecological production of truths, as much as why they may not.

Epiphanies of Evidence

Latour's effort to pluralise the way scholars distribute agency – in this case specifically how they read everyday investments in fact – folds back on itself by dividing forms of inquiry and comment, while at the same time affirming the public's taste for ideology critique and critique's capacity for concern. The foundation Sedgwick uses to verify her turn from critique is equally provocative. Sedgwick begins her career as a queer theorist, finely attuned to the productive persuasion of cultural narratives and dedicated to uncovering the heteronormative implications of their reproduction. Her field-defining studies, such as *Between Men: English Literature and Male Homosocial Desire* (1985) and *Epistemology of the Closet* (1990), popularised a revelatory methodology in queer theory that sought to draw out the complex sexualities hidden in canonical works of literature. But after a series of unique personal events and developments, Sedgwick decides that such work is no longer germane. However, as with Latour, when we look closely at Sedgwick's testimony about this conversion, the evidence used to verify a turn *from* paranoid reading *to* reparative reading actually draws out both the inextricability and ambiguity of these modes.

Sedgwick outlines her turn against critique in an essay that first appeared as the introduction to *Novel Gazing: Queer Readings in Fiction* (1997). In the boldly titled, 'You're So Paranoid You Probably Think This Introduction Is About You: Paranoid Reading and Reparative Reading' (1997), Sedgwick argues that the essays collected in *Novel Gazing* present a new precedent for how to read texts. Marking their promise as a departure from the hermeneutics of suspicion, Sedgwick explains that 'aside from the deroutinizing methodologies of these essays, what seems most hauntingly to characterise them is how distant many of them are from a certain stance of suspicion or paranoia that is common in the disciplinary work whose ambience surrounds them' (3).

Sedgwick's intervention favours an earthier engagement with quotidian forms of attention. Initially, her project leavens out its field and emphasises inclusion. Sedgwick tries to think through a way to register the lived, everyday texture of her own practice, and specifically the modes by which it is driven and verified. 'Suppose one takes seriously a notion', she considers:

> that everyday theory qualitatively affects everyday knowledge and experience; [. . .] that one doesn't want to draw much ontological distinction between academic theory and everyday theory; and [. . .] has a lot of concern for the quality of other people's and one's own practices of knowing and experiencing. (20)

Her project aims to be self-reflexive and extends its generosity to other scholars. When Sedgwick praises the work of the essays collected in *Novel Gazing*, for instance, it is because: 'Though passionate, they are also not particularly polemical, and they don't greatly feature the disciplining of previous errors of theory or interpretation' (1).

In several of its opening considerations and aims Sedgwick's proposal is inspiring: the desire to consider 'academic theory' as 'everyday theory', or to engage with past interventions rather than dismissing them as erroneous. It offers a less caustic and divisive approach to contemporary methodological ethics, one we might use specifically to re-gauge the possibilities of critique. However, despite this sensitive outline of the problems and promise of critical intervention, when we look closely at the continuation of Sedgwick's argument, particularly as she sets up reparative reading as a correction to paranoid reading, it is clear that her own method remains 'polemical' and 'corrective of previous errors of theory and interpretation' (1).

For Sedgwick, paranoid reading, or 'the frequent privileging of paranoid methodologies in [...] feminist theory, psychoanalytic theory, deconstruction, Marxist criticism, or the New Historicism', is out of date (7). In a line of reasoning that appears to preserve the methods of New Historicism at the same time as it declares the task of tracing ideological formations outmoded, Sedgwick posits Cold War paranoia as the genesis of paranoid reading, which she explains is now an engrained schema being routinely applied to a world it no longer suits. Noting 'a popular maxim of the late 1960s', Sedgwick reasons:

> it seems quite plausible to me that some version of this axiom ['Just because you're paranoid doesn't mean they're not out to get you'] is so indelibly inscribed in the brains of us baby boomers that it offers us the continuing illusion of possessing a special insight into the epistemologies of enmity. (7)

Sedgwick explains that events like the Watergate scandal reinforced paranoid critique because they vindicated conspiracy theory. 'In a world where no one need be delusional to find evidence of systematic oppression', Sedgwick suggests, 'to theorize out of anything but a paranoid critical stance has come to seem naive, pious, or complaisant' (Sedgwick 1997: 5).

This is a problem for Sedgwick because paranoid reading, in addition to being untimely, is beset by essential limitations that render it incapable of achieving her intended generosity. Noting a 'property of paranoia itself', Sedgwick argues that it is 'contagious'. She also 'explains' that it is anticipatory and intrinsically pessimistic:

> The first imperative of paranoia is 'There must be no bad surprises', [...] because there must be no bad surprises, and because to learn of the possibility of a bad surprise would itself constitute a bad surprise, paranoia requires that bad news be always already known. (9)

Paranoid reading, in Sedgwick's definition, is pre-emptive and retaliatory: 'Paranoia proposes both "Anything you can do [to me] I can do worse", and "Anything you can do [to me] I can do first" – to myself' (9). The method is limited, according to Sedgwick, in its perception and response, like a monotonous reflex involuntarily responding to all stimuli with the same knee-jerk reaction.

Critique is caricatured here. In Sedgwick's description, the apparently limited nature of critique is not based on evidence from specific texts. We do not see examples of critics rigidly trying to apply Cold War logic to contemporary questions. Rather, 'Paranoid Reading', as a proper noun, is given its own unappealing persona as a natural antagonist. Isolating the critical method as the bad seed of contemporary theory, Sedgwick contends: it is 'only paranoid knowledge that has so thorough a practice of disavowing its affective motive and force, and masquerading as the very stuff of truth' (15). Sedgwick also presents paranoid reading as a deterrent to other more positive forms of inquiry. '[T]he mushrooming, self- confirming strength of a monopolistic strategy of anticipating negative affect can have [...] the effect', she argues, 'of entirely blocking the potentially operative goal of seeking positive affect' (14, emphasis added). Like Latour, Sedgwick also displays a conspiracist tone when she represents 'paranoid reading' as a malignant growth threatening to subsume scholarly practice:

> If there is an obvious danger in the triumphalism of a paranoid hermeneutic, it is that the broad consensual sweep of such methodological assumptions, the current near-profession-wide agreement about what constitutes narrative or explanation or adequate historicization, may, if it persists unquestioned, unintentionally impoverish the gene pool of literary-critical perspectives and skills. The trouble with a narrow gene pool, of course, is its diminished ability to respond to environmental (for instance, political) change. (21)

Akin to Latour's military crisis metaphor, Sedgwick's biological crisis creates an alarming atmosphere, forewarning imminent disaster and political paralysis.

In this climate, it is fair to say not only that paranoid reading, a term representative of diverse methods, seems exempt from Sedgwick's reparation, but also that Sedgwick herself, anticipating and forewarning, remains implicated in this method, even on her own terms. Paranoid reading poses a threat of which to be wary. As Heather Love has argued, 'despite the methodological gains and affective appeal of the turn away from critique' she does not 'think it's possible to read Sedgwick's essay on paranoid and reparative reading as only a call for reparative reading' (Love 2010: 238). Love asserts that '[t]here is no doubt [Sedgwick] extends this call. But that is not all she does [. . .] the essay itself is not only reparative – it is paranoid' (238). We are therefore met with the paradox that Sedgwick chooses a paranoid method to argue for reparation, to make a positive intervention, despite her claim that this method is incapable of such a feat.

Again, the lack of citation to exemplify critique proves telling, as if to include critique itself might bring 'a bad surprise' or complicate the coherence of reform. Indeed, could this lack of specific citation from critical texts – evidence needed to prove critique is essentially paranoid, out-of-date and dismissive – be explained by the fact that critical work, when held up for scrutiny, does not actually fit, and thus support, such a narrow description? The one example Sedgwick selectively cites as an example of the paranoid method in queer theory is D. A. Miller's *The Novel and The Police* (1988). But even with this example, one she has chosen for the task, Sedgwick struggles to exemplify her point. When she describes the specific nature of Miller's writing, she concedes that it does not conform to the particular polemic she has outlined. When describing its grim 'strong theory', its affective inflexibility (opposed to the preferred 'weak theory'), she explains:

[T]he very breadth of reach that makes the theory strong also offers the space – of which this book takes every advantage – for a wealth of tonal nuance, attitude, worldly observation, performative paradox, aggression, tenderness, wit, inventive reading, obiter dicta, and writerly panache. These rewards are so local and frequent that one might want to say that a plethora of only loosely related weak theories has been invited to shelter in the hypertrophied embrace of the book's overarching strong theory. In many ways, such an arrangement is all to the good – suggestive, pleasurable, and highly productive; an insistence that everything means one thing somehow permits a sharpened sense of all the ways there are of meaning it. (14)

Allowing, then, that the book is affectively flexible, that it lends and inspires all manner of emotional engagements with its texts and readers, Sedgwick must explain how the text is read as paranoid despite this.

To circumscribe Miller's text as a model, Sedgwick argues that his work, despite its obvious multimodality and nuance, is read only for its 'grim' narrative of Victorian literature's role in reproducing conservative, hetero-normative sexual identities:

> But one need not read an infinite number of students' and other critics' derivative rephrasings of the book's grimly strong theory to see, as well, some limitations of this unarticulated relation between strong and weak theories. As strong theory, and as a locus of reflexive mimeticism, paranoia is nothing if not teachable. The powerfully ranging and reductive force of strong theory can make tautological thinking hard to identify, even as it makes it compelling and near-inevitable; the result is that both writers and readers can damagingly misrecognize whether and where real conceptual work is getting done and precisely what that work might be. (15)

Because Sedgwick requires that Miller is only read grimly, because she 'anticipates' an always already 'bad surprise', Miller's noted, and intriguing, defiance of the strong/weak is elided. With the qualification that all who read his book will grossly reduce its message – a claim that crosses Sedgwick's driving claim that 'popular cynicism, while undoubtedly widespread, is only one among the heterogeneous, competing theories that constitute the mental ecology of most people' (17) – we are meant to take Miller's text as proof that paranoid reading is grim and that Sedgwick's reparative reading provides a more generous method. But as Sedgwick's text infers, Miller's critique is not wholly paranoid and Sedgwick's is not wholly reparative. There is a tension within these methods that challenges their oppositional descriptions.

The way Sedgwick verifies her critique offers insight into the contingency of the critical method as a living struggle of fact and value. When setting up the division between paranoid and reparative reading, Sedgwick motions towards their differing relations to truth value. Marking her project's interest in unverifiable truths, she claims the essays of *Novel Gazing* are valuable because they reveal 'that an ethic or aesthetic of truthtelling need not depend on any reified notion of truth' (1). Paranoid reading, in contrast, is geared towards unveiling, or reifying, hidden truths. But in the development of Sedgwick's critical position, clear distinctions between factual and felt truths are difficult to locate. Her critique, for instance, is verified with a series of personal epiphanies, lived experiences and social interpretations.

However, this does not mean that for Sedgwick these facts, the motor of her critique, are not reified. This subjective data are used as a generalisable fact with which to justify a definitive, field-wide shift in method. However, as with Miller's critique, Sedgwick does not lend evidence to the strict and essential division of affect and critique. The means by which her argument is leveraged confounds such terms. Critique is not removed from the precarious values of life, but contests and participates in their very reproduction.

Citing her critical turning point, Sedgwick explains that her reassessment of paranoid reading was provoked by an exchange with her friend, the activist and scholar Cindy Patton, about the origin of HIV. Sedgwick (1997), struck by ubiquitous speculation about whether 'the virus had been deliberately engineered, or spread; whether HIV represented a plot or experiment by the U.S. government which had gotten out of control, or perhaps was behaving exactly as it was meant to', approached Patton to ask her what she made of 'these sinister rumours' (5). Sedgwick was startled by her friend's response, which, unlike her own keen interest in getting to the bottom of all the speculation, was indifferent to the disease's origin. Patton argued that she saw little pragmatic worth in the possible revelation of such knowledge:

> [E]ven suppose we are sure of every element of a conspiracy: that the lives of Africans and African Americans are worthless in the eyes of the United States; that gay men and drug users are held cheap where they aren't actively hated; that the military deliberately researches ways to kill noncombatants ... supposing we were ever so sure of all those things – what would we know then that we don't already know? (Patton, cited in Sedgwick 1997: 5)

Sedgwick explains that this statement was a catalyst for her: it helped her unpack 'the intellectual baggage that many of us carry around under a label like "the hermeneutic of suspicion"' (3). Sedgwick decided that her academic practice need not be based on the question of 'is a particular piece of knowledge true', but '[w]hat does knowledge do?' (5).

Sedgwick's point of departure is interesting because she decides to move away from a methodology of exposure, and in doing so does not question whether her friend's premise itself is necessarily cogent, or true, or socially representative. She emphasises a turn to pragmatism, but seems to assume that the pursuit of these truths is not already pragmatically motivated. There is an important difference between whether a disease is a naturally mutated phenomenon and whether it was a deliberate act of systemic genocide. It is questionable whether this information would have little utility or effect. The revelation of the Holocaust death camps, surely of comparable horror to the suggestion of this more recent fascist genocide if it were true, certainly could not be said to have had no important constitutive political, historical or social effects – not to *do* anything. It may not be of interest to Patton, but to suggest that the revelation of this would be of little utility in general, and to take this statement as the reason to move away from an academic practice of uncovering factual oversights and political quietisms, seems unjustified.

Sedgwick makes a similarly testimonial argument in 'Melanie Klein and the Difference Affect Makes' (2007), again presenting a personal and intuited account of why suspicion is no longer an appropriate orientation towards political reality. To begin, Sedgwick argues that, particularly in her field of queer theory, the guiding theoretical force of paranoia was justified in 'the 1980s and early 1990s' by the fear and discrimination of the AIDS epidemic, by 'the not knowing what kind of response to AIDS might crystallize from the state or public sphere' (638). Sedgwick (2007) captures the palpable sense of impending terror the queer community felt at that historical moment, when 'prominent legislators and complacent pundits busied themselves with fake-judicious, fake-practical, prurient schemes for testing, classifying, rounding up, tattooing, quarantining, and otherwise demeaning and killing men and women with AIDS' (639). Sedgwick explains that 'the

punishing stress, of such dread, and the need for mobilizing powerful resources of resistance in the face of it, did imprint a paranoid
structuration onto the theory and activism of that period, and
no wonder' (639). From this perspective, Sedgwick shifts slightly
to reassess the calamity in hindsight. 'Now we live in a world in
which most of these things haven't happened, at least in relation
to AIDS', but at that time, 'there was no visible brake on [the]
implementation [of discriminatory legislation] from any sanc-
tioned, nonhomo-phobic argument in the public sphere' (639). As
a result, 'the congruence of such fantasies [. . .] with Foucauldian
understandings of how panoptic power gets embodied through
the disciplines of bureaucracy, law, psychiatry, science, and public
health, was inescapable to those who awaited or fought to prevent
their implementation' (639). In these passages, Sedgwick illustrates
that queer theory was justifiably suspicious, and poststructural, in
its battle to draw out the murderousness in protectionist, homo-
phobic rhetoric that was (and arguably still is), reproduced in
certain social structures and institutions. Critique, as a means to
wrestle with these forces, was welcomed in the humanities as a
consequence.

However, Sedgwick explains that, in 'the mid-1990s', 'developments both public and private came together, for [her], to produce
some changed relations to paranoid thinking and writing' (639).
'A nodal point', she states, was the revelation that AIDS could be
medically treated and the life of its sufferers prolonged (639). As
a result, Sedgwick explains that: 'Along with many, many others,
[she] was trying over that summer to assimilate an unaccustomed
palette of feelings among which relief, hope, and expansiveness and
surprise set the tone' (639). At the same time, Sedgwick learns she
has advanced breast cancer. Reckoning with her illness, she suspects
that her 'lifelong depressiveness' has made her 'perhaps oversensitive
to the psychic expense exhorted by the paranoid defences' (640).
With regard to her own health, Sedgwick states 'I knew for sure
that the paranoid/schizoid was no place I could afford to dwell as I
dealt with the exigencies of my disease' (640). Summating the basis
of these two personal shifts – an improvement in the prospects for
people living with AIDS and her decision, in the face of illness, to
depart from what she feels to be a draining practice – Sedgwick

states that: 'At any rate, for reasons both private and public, I found myself at this point increasingly discontented with the predominance of the self-perpetuating kinds of thought that I increasingly seemed to be recognizing under the rubric of paranoia' (640). It is for these very subjective reasons, based on a need to conserve her energy and her sense of relief as AIDS became less stigmatised and threatening, that Sedgwick instigates a turn away from paranoid reading and critique.

Nonetheless, Sedgwick's personal conversion is also presented as an instructive precedent for queer theory, for she states that the paranoid zeitgeist is outmoded not only for her but for the field generally. She argues that: 'A lot of more recent queer theory has retained the paranoid structure of the earlier AIDS years, but done so increasingly outside of a context where it had reflected a certain, palpable purchase on daily reality' (640). Based on her own particular intellectual and activist project, Sedgwick's shift is understandable; however, it is important to consider what is implicit in her reflection that '[n]ow we live in a world in which most of these things haven't happened, *at least in relation to AIDS*' (639, emphasis added). Sedgwick does not pursue this qualification; however, it is vital to recognise that the anxieties she argues are no longer evident in the queer community do remain relevant to other groups facing social scapegoating and discrimination. In this context, a sense of political paranoia, and the desire to critically intervene or to challenge dominant ideologies and systemic inequality, does retain 'a certain palpable purchase on daily reality' (640). Suspicion remains vital in an arena where what constitutes and sustains a fact is both contingent and contested.

There may be truth to Sedgwick's observation that the queer community is no longer stigmatised and threatened to the extent that it was in the 1980s, at least in the West. Certainly there was a fever-pitch of moral panic at this time, when the Australian government, for instance, screened a horrifying AIDS prevention ad campaign featuring a scythe-wielding grim reaper and forewarning – with a voice-over citing projective statistics and footage of dead bodies piling up in the mist – of an impending death count to rival the Holocaust. This level of public hysteria around AIDS has abated. However, as a reaction to the terrorist attacks of 9/11, or the global rise of nationalist populism, new sets of people have become the target of moral panic – indeed we could re-use the very terms Sedgwick uses in reference to the 1980s to describe the kind of logic that supported extraordinary rendition policies during the Iraq war. In this case, 'prominent legislators and complacent pundits busied themselves with fake-judicious, fake-practical, prurient schemes for [. . .] classifying, rounding up, quarantining, and otherwise demeaning' (638–9) people they deem to have no civil rights, not on the basis of potential infection, but on the basis of their religion, nationality and familial or political affiliations. In this context, though Sedgwick may claim that the critical desire to examine causal connections and uncover injustice is no longer valuable to her, she cannot justifiably claim that it has no political purchase in general. It is worth noting that the European Union's reports on the US government's extraordinary rendition policies, revealing secret government acts including the inter-country transport and unlawful detention and torture of people, were released and highly publicised in 2006 and 2007, the year leading up to the publication of Sedgwick's article.

As both Latour's and Sedgwick's arguments demonstrate, what verifies a critical turn does not have to be logically coherent and carefully verified: knowledge is actualised by facts, rhetoric, assumptions, intuitions, projections and other contingent forms of evidence. Despite the nature of both Latour's and Sedgwick's points of departure, each a reactive and subjective reading of political reality, their experiences leverage a dramatic and influential departure in methodology – ostensibly from suspicion and facts to reparation and concern. However, the detail of these arguments prove that both scholarly and social methods demand more nuance than such polemical limitations allow, and yet the question of why a hermeneutics of suspicion has become prominent in both academic and social forms of inquiry is set aside in favour of a new slate. Critique, in its incurable paranoia, is represented as irreparable and unworthy of concern.

Such arguments against critique install a resolute, moral opposition between pessimistic and optimistic methods, even though to do so works against their efforts to rethink divisive structures of knowing. In his 'Compositionist Manifesto' (2010), for instance, Latour offers compositionism as the moral diametric of critique. Composition emerges not as a clear method but as a general orientation against critique, though Latour states that he likes the term because 'it has clear roots in art, painting, music, theater, dance, and thus is associated with choreography and scenography' (474). His argument is that in order to be ethical we must be caring, and in order to do this we must use methods of creation instead of what he sees to be critique's innate destructiveness (473). Latour reiterates his earlier position, arguing that critique has expired:

> To be sure, critique did a wonderful job of debunking preju- dices, enlightening nations, prodding minds, but, as I have argued elsewhere, it 'ran out of steam' because it was predicated on the discovery of a true world of realities lying behind a veil of appearances. (Latour 2010: 475)

Making a polemical distinction between critique and composition, he argues that '*what performs a critique cannot also compose*' (475). In refer- ence to one of Ricœur's masters of suspicion, Friedrich Nietzsche's *Twilight of the Idols, Or, How to Philosophise with a Hammer* ([1888] 1986), Latour explains that, '[w]ith a hammer (or a sledge hammer) in hand you can do a lot of things: break down walls, destroy idols, ridicule prejudices, but you cannot repair, take care, assemble, reas- semble, stitch together' (475). However, the broader social context of Latour's project, his desire to move beyond Cold War paranoia, begins precisely with a hammer, as the destruction of the Berlin Wall ushered in the end of the Cold War and was, for some, the first step both in assembling peace and stitching Europe back together. Nonetheless, Latour deems it 'necessary to move from iconoclasm to [...] the *suspension* of the critical impulse [...]' (475).

While there is evidence to locate paranoia, although not exclu- sively, within the Cold War era, little more than a personal fatigue with criticism is offered to justify why our current age demands a radically different, and allegedly more hopeful and credulous, approach. Indeed, when we look at other work on paranoia, it is not clear that suspicion is a redundant or unwarranted reaction, precisely because the means by which knowledge is actualised are unpredict- able and insecure. It is the fickle and fluid nature of political rhetoric and modes of interpretation that keep people in a permanent state of vigilance. As Marita Sturken explains, 'we have moved from various phases of late modern optimism into cold-war fears, from 1960s disillusion to a late twentieth-century culture in which conspiracy theory forms a primary narrative' (1997: 64). Discussing the prevalence of paranoid themes in twenty-first-century literature, Emily Apter also argues that paranoia is a response as relevant now as it was in the Cold War period. 'Now, as then,' she argues, 'paranoia assumes the guise of a delusional democracy buoyed by cascading national cataclysms: the Bay of Pigs, the Kennedy and King assassinations, Kent State, the FBI hunt for Black Panthers, Symbionese Liberation Army and Weather Underground radicals, Watergate, Iran-Contra, Waco, Oklahoma City, Columbine, and 9/11' (Apter 2006: 368). Taking up the most recent of these events, Apter explains that, '[p]aranoia has returned with a vengeance as the ordre du jour in the aftermath of 9/11' (369).

Contrary to Sedgwick's argument that paranoia is a remnant of the political past, Apter argues that in the aftermath of this 9/11, the American citizen has been 'exhorted by Washington to connect the dots, to posit connections between weapons of mass destruction in Iraq and the world trade center attacks' (369). Apter adds to this that:

> In this scheme, what we are told *is* connected is rivalled only by what we are asked to believe is *not* connected: there is apparently *no* link between oil and the Iraq invasion, *no* coincidence between electioneering politics and war, *no* cause-effect relationship between the media-hyped epistemology of insecurity and the abrogation of civil liberties. (369)

To Apter's account we could add more recent cases such as the exposé of torture and prisoner abuse at Abu Ghraib or the ongoing Wikileaks scandals. Is paranoid reading truly inappropriate when the public learns in 2013, via the whistle-blowing former CIA and NSA computer technician Edward Snowdon that the United States of America's National Security Agency, operating a mass surveillance network, can access and monitor the social-networking accounts, emails, Word documents, video-chats, file transfers and browsing history of both US and non-US citizens at any time without court approval? In the political climate that Apter describes here, where a complex state of paranoia is almost a prerequisite of citizenship, it is clear why the zeitgeist is, in this time, as paranoid as ever and why a hermeneutics of suspicion remains pertinent. As I will turn to in Chapter 5, the advent of fake news, the dark web and the revelation of social media data manipulation for political purposes by companies such as Cambridge Analytica continue to justify this mode of attention. We are confronted daily with stories of this enduring political reality. Where people have to deal daily with a lack of transparency, it is little wonder that they are suspicious. The assumption that social scientists should somehow be immune to such shifts, or indeed position themselves outside them, deserves to be treated with some suspicion also.

In *Paranoia Within Reason* (1999), George Marcus wishes to 'come to terms with the paranoid style, not as distanced from the "really" rational [. . .] but *within reason*, as a "reasonable" component of rational and commonsensical thought and experience in certain contexts' (Marcus 1999: 2). Marcus and Sedgwick see the Cold War legacy of paranoia in markedly different ways: Marcus sees the legacy in the fact that people could no longer trust their governments, whereas Sedgwick sees the legacy as the tyrannical suspicion of McCarthy himself. But of course both positions were inherent and instrumental to the same political reality. It is the fact that people, like Sedgwick and Marcus, experience and interpret facts and their consequences in very different ways that is at stake in this discussion. It is difficult to draw a rigid line between or singularly adjudicate the validity of matters of fact and matters of concern. The experiential moment that Sedgwick uses as evidence for her turn away from critique, her revelation that the true cause of AIDS is not necessarily a productive piece of knowledge, may not necessarily be sound evidence to someone else. As both Sedgwick's and Latour's testimonies illustrate, suspicion is vital in an arena where what constitutes a fact is both contingent and contested.

Pessimism is not inherent to critique itself, but rather to a narrow definition of it. The suggestion that we rescind our suspicion is problematic precisely because the negativity of critique, the desire to hear what is silenced and to consider its productive force, is not inherently pessimistic or lacking in creativity. Suspicion can also be pedagogical, protective, enabling and caring. Latour argues that to progress in scholarship we must become 'caring', but to care about something might mean to fight for it, to be both defensive and judicious. A censorious attitude to critique in the name of social ethics does not account for how vital critical faculties are to the everyday citizen as a means to participate in democracy, the law and the market, forums that require us to navigate and often challenge rhetoric and our involvement in its structuring force on a day-to-day basis. The field-defining arguments of Latour and Sedgwick summon several very important questions about the continuing power of ideology and thus ideology critique. However, these questions are prematurely set aside, and even stigmatised, when Sedgwick, for example, likens the paranoid critic to 'the deinstitutionalized person on the street who, betrayed and plotted against by everyone else in the city, still urges on you the finger-worn dossier bristling with his precious correspondence' (1997: 17). A turn from critique to affect may mock scholars who remain faithful to critical methods, but this does not obscure the fact that such arguments often remain invested in these very questions and ideals. Latour and Sedgwick point to ideologies, they critique their scholarly precedents, they represent society on both macro and micro levels, and they argue for superior methods. The critique of critique is an exercise in exactly what it claims to depart from. It is a self-assured diagnostic about what narratives should qualify as truthful, factual, valuable or authentic, and it claims exclusive insight into the realities of social attachment. As I have shown thus far, these arguments do not work in favour of their set aims, namely to be inclusive or reparative. To engage further with the turn against critique and its implications, we must next consider what is at stake in this contradiction of aims.

Productive Blind Spots

The 'critique of critique' has a blind spot regarding its own hermeneutics of suspicion. But again, in Sedgwick's terms, errors remain productive. Latour and Sedgwick, like Felski and Massumi, dismiss suspicion and judiciousness, but their narratives remain paranoid. By their own accounts, they are besieged; what they hold dear both politically and professionally is threatened. Paranoid reading, in this context, is not a rigid and bygone method. Neither is critique immune to affect. As these calls demonstrate, the impetus of criticism is often concern – both personal and passionate. Critique's drive, as illustrated here, is social, embodied, emotional, impelled by hit nerves and the rattle of everyday encounters with people and colleagues. Latour and Sedgwick defer to personal epiphanies about the redundancy of paranoia for their proposed change in method. And yet their use of conversion narratives – mixed in with history, science and intuition – structures and verifies their arguments in a way that challenges the opposition of what is felt and what is factual. These influential theorists assume a strict division between ideology critique and affective experience, but the mixed methodology that animates their own arguments works against this easy discrimination. It demonstrates that what we take to be the verifying factor of a certain narrative is not necessarily either facts *or* values but often something much less distinct.

What this generic diffusion suggests is not that veracity is of little value, but that one can never be sure what will be counted as evidence: in some cases what is clearly questionable serves as concrete proof. In the critical proposals discussed, experience, no less than any other kind of empirical evidence, verifies and justifies a bold departure in methodology. The fact that Sedgwick's moment of realisation (her chat with Cindy Patton) is problematic does not mean that her testimony has not compelled an entire field of research on affect and on reparative methods. The point is that it has had an enormous impact precisely because Sedgwick's critical intervention into literature, culture and politics is both incisive and impassioned. Sedgwick's writing is cynical, satirical and audacious. It mixes, in the written critical genre, felt and detected truths to verify a vital point of relational and intellectual contact. Paranoia animates Sedgwick's reparation and matters of fact provoke Latour's matter of concern. While the field-defining theorists discussed do not ultimately achieve the inclusive, ethical solution to the difficulty of representing social life that they propose, they do add to the intricacy of this issue by demonstrating that even those critics claiming to extricate themselves remain invested in the generativity of critique. These theorists are not willing to exchange the revelatory for the ineffable – to follow through with the pragmatic implications of their moral arguments about truth-seeking methods. They too are vying to position their account as the *most* authentic. They too have a stake in making a judgement about which narratives do and do not have value.

With attention to these proposals, this chapter has amplified questions about the constitution of veracity, the nature of evidence, and the efficacy of suspicion that are at risk of being censored. Rather than simply demonstrating that these field-defining scholars rely on the positivist, epistemological trope of evidentiary reference they discourage, a close analysis of their means of verification questions whether their continued reliance on this reflex, as well as a tangle of others, actually undermines the basis upon which we discriminate and separate different genres of social inquiry.

Close analysis of these directives for a turn against critique, and their paradoxical formation, challenges us not to drift with the current of the critical moment, but rather to consider what is implicit in its momentum. As Avery Gordon explains of critical turns, new avenues open but there is also always the question of 'what paths have been disavowed, left behind, covered over and remain unseen' (2008: 41). Here we see the implications of such omissions. For instance, identifying genres as bald caricatures, with intrinsic and polemic moral values – such as Latour's 'critique' versus 'composition' – makes it difficult to engage generously with how people might use genre to wrangle an authentic account of themselves or the world. The scholarly reversal of the fact/affect hierarchy similarly overlooks the question of how genres, methods and disciplines, are constituted and what role they play in determining the truth-value of one account over another. This static conception of genres' structure does not acknowledge how genre itself is a contingent and changeable form. Paranoia, or a 'hermeneutics of suspicion', is assumed to have no affective potential or only a de(con)structive one. Thus my aim – to complicate the fact/affect division with close attention to how it is verified – is important not only for my own argument, but also for the arguments that inform the critique of critique, which aims to capture life in its complexity. Returning to the words of Bernhard Schlink, it 'is of crucial importance that we don't make this world simpler than it is' (BBC 2011) by casting the identity and intentions of people, or in this case methods, as simply malignant or benign. Every utterance of every genre is socially informed and productive in various ways.

The theorists discussed here genuinely aim to stimulate an ethical and political re-evaluation of the scholar's role in social debate. Though Latour and Sedgwick motion toward the utopia of new genres, they re-enlist critical method to mobilise their political interventions. These arguments themselves indicate that the nature of evidence *and* interpretation remain entangled and unsure, and the scholar, in the face of such a hermeneutic challenge, still seeks to wrest sense, purpose and an ever-clearer insight into how life is authored. In the proposals discussed in this chapter the polemic between affect-driven, lived experience and the ratio of verifiable evidence is constantly unsettled. This highlights the ongoing utility of critical genres and faculties and encourages us to rethink the idea that the hermeneutics of suspicion is no longer salient. The sense that we must be engaged and vigilant, or that meaning can be wrestled from the ineffable, remains the unacknowledged motivation of the critique of critique. With this in mind, perhaps there is a different lesson to be learnt about the possibilities of critical methods from these arguments. Addressing the persistence of distrust and guardedness within this turn, could we perhaps open up critique as a broader social phenomenon that is neither easily located nor excised? The question, in these terms, would not be how to surpass the hermeneutics of suspicion, but rather why it remains such a pervasive form of social interpretation, even in the work of its critics.

3

The Crisis of 'Non-Representation'

Despite the complex and provocative nature of their formulation, arguments against critique, with their advocacy for affect-oriented alternatives, have inspired a collection of method proposals. Cultural geographer Nigel Thrift's 'non-representational theory' (2007) and sociologist John Law's 'mess as method' (2004) are two very influential examples. Parallel to this, related arguments have endorsed various manifestations of 'creative methods' as alternatives to critical essays (Muecke 2002 and 2010; Stewart 2007; Taussig 2010). In the way they are framed, some of these method directives, as I will detail here, work with the notion that genres are essentially enabling *or* disabling. Genres that might be associated with emotional truth, such as creative writing or performance, are pursued and promoted as better avenues for social research because they are seen to be *of* the dynamic substance of the world. Critique, alternatively, is cast as a method of observation that imposes from outside, inevitably reducing the mutable complexity of social phenomena. Reiterating the 'two cultures' divide, this shift from critical to artistic methods is framed as an ethical imperative: firstly, as a responsibility to knowledge – to keep our methods relevant; and secondly, as a social responsibility – to access what really matters to people.

Taking these same responsibilities into account, this chapter carefully considers the terms of this proposed shift, as well as how we might determine what is distinctly affective about certain genres and not others. Several important questions arise. For instance, might the distribution of suspicion or truth-value among different forms of representation be more complex than either a critical or creative approach alone can accommodate? Are the genres we read as 'creative' really more expressive and emotional or less definitive and didactic than critique? And do fictive forms truly provide an antidote or reprieve from the political quandaries of the culture wars or the suspicious taint of the Cold War era? In sum, are the determinants of this turn in method – both the intellectual history from which it claims to depart and the raw, everyday desires it claims to access – really as different in tenor and drive as these method proposals assume?

In this chapter I show that even a cursory look into the central themes of literature and popular culture in the late twentieth and early twenty-first centuries – specifically in the Western centres where these scholars are located – suggests that poststructural questions and hermeneutic methods are a central driver of creative works. Indeed, a strong body of research contends that paranoia has become *the* pinnacle theme of postmodern literature, demonstrated by key figures in the literary canon, such as Phillip Roth, Thomas Pynchon, Don DeLillo, Margaret Atwood, Kathy Acker, Patricia Highsmith, George Orwell and others (Bersani 1989; Melley 2000; Fenster 2008; Trask 2010; Auper 2012). In *Empire of Conspiracy: The Culture of Paranoia in Post-war America* (2000), Timothy Melley explains that writers as different as these have 'depicted individuals nervous about the ways large organisations might be controlling their lives, influencing their actions, or even constructing their desires' (2000: xii). In this light, we can reconsider the position that paranoid thinking is a Cold War malaise that only affects a torpid ivory tower, as the congruence of paranoid themes across scholarly and popular forms of narration suggests a different story. Read this way, I argue here, we might see suspicion *across genres* as an expression of a broader social zeitgeist.

To begin the discussion, I puzzle through several methods proposals focusing specifically on why they deem certain genres to be more creative than others and therefore more in touch with social life. This discussion will draw out some of the intellectual and ethical issues that arise from how these method proposals represent the project of social science, the project of creative practice, and the public culture they hope to better engage. With a fuller social context for these method proposals, it becomes clear that unresolved questions about what determines the value of particular genres is still very much alive within cultural theory and society at large. In this light, I conclude that we need a more detailed picture of what is at stake in evaluating genres on the basis of received notions about their capacity to affect.

New Vocations?

Thrift's *Non-Representational Theory: Space, Politics, Affect* (2007) proposes a social science method that 'concentrate[s] on *practices*' (12), aims to be 'experimental' (8) and 're-gather[s] the ethic of *craftsmanship*' (15). He argues that these creative methods are better suited to what the social world currently demands of social scientists, namely to engage with the affective, dynamic and post-human. Thus he argues that non-representation, as opposed to representation, can 'capture the "onflow" […] of everyday life' (5), trade in 'modes of perception which are not subject-based' but rather 'resolutely anti-biographical and pre-individual' (7) and 'get in touch with the full range of registers of thought by stressing affect and sensation' (12). His act of promoting the creative arts is accompanied by a demotion of current social science practices. With a simultaneous act of advocacy and admonition, Thrift argues that 'the performing arts can have as much rigour as any other experimental set up, once it is understood that the laboratory, and all the models that have resulted from it, provide much too narrow a metaphor to be able to capture the richness of the worlds' (12). He suggests that 'the performing arts may help us to inject a note of wonder back into a social science which, too often, assumes that it must explain everything' (12). With these assessments, Thrift contributes to the broad characterisation of existing social analysis that we have seen in the arguments discussed so far, namely that it is stale and impolitic.

   For Thrift the turn is a necessary and ethical act. He argues that, '[w]e are continually being made into new creatures by all kinds of forces, but it is surely the case that as the world is forced to face up to the damage done, so we can no longer move along the same cul-de-sacs of practical-cum-conceptual possibilities' (Thrift 2007: vii). Thrift offers 'non-representational theory' as a response to this call for change and argues that it can better attune itself to the speed of social and political dynamics. To position traditional scholarly genres as unsuitable for this task, Thrift evokes the language of Brian Massumi, describing the presence of autonomous forces which are impervious to representation. He states that 'it is imperative to understand the virtual as multiple registers of sensation operating beyond the reach of the reading techniques on which the social sciences are founded' (12). In the light of the revelation of how 'affective forces' work, Thrift suggests we can no longer characterise social life with traditional representational forms. Instead, '[o]ther possibilities need to be alighted on for thinking about the world. That requires boosting inventive attitude so as to produce more contrary motion' (vii). Thrift argues that his non-representational theory provides these other possibilities because it is not representational and thus not hindered by the stubborn solipsism he attributes to critical essays and data sets.

In Thrift's presentation of creative practices as a superior vocation to existing forms of scholarship, we see the dismissiveness that provokes the protective tone of existing critiques of the affective turn (Hemmings 2006; Papoulias and Callard 2010; and Leys 2011). To champion creativity and practice, Thrift unnecessarily trivialises criticality and erudition. He argues that a 'more valuable endeavour' than social science would be 'to try to construct *practices* of vocation' (3). In turning to 'practice', Thrift explains that he 'want[s] to try and add a distinct co-operative-cum-experimental sensibility in to the mix of the world that will help us "engage the strangeness of the late modern world more receptively"' (Thrift 2007: 4). He suggests that '[t]he net outcome would be that the texture of the feel and outcome of the everyday could be reworked as traditional forms of expression were slowly but surely breathed differently' (4). Although academics may see their existing labour, as researchers, writers and teachers, to be vocational, Thrift implores that we must look outside the social sciences for evidence of this model. The next question then, if we are to consider Thrift's methodological shift, is what the practice of 'non-representational theory' actually entails? What marks its radical break with current practices? What, in short, makes it better?

The answer to this question seems as opaque as its premise. Social scientists are asked to give up their existing disciplinary practices for 'co-operative-cum-experimental' methods without contextualised detail about the proposed alternatives and why they qualify as superior. If Thrift were simply opening up new forms of research, this might not be of concern: not all research has to conform to the strictures of critical theory. What makes the diffuseness of this proposal troublesome, however, is that it is offered as a *correction* to the naivety of other methods. Thrift's ideal template for a 'practice of vocation' is dance. He argues: 'dance is important: it engages the whole of the senses in bending time and space in new kinaesthetic shapes [. . .], challenges the privileging of meaning, gives weight to intuition as thinking-in-movement' (Thrift 2007: 14). He adds that although 'my stomping ground for these kinds of thoughts has often been dance, [. . .] it could just as well be building or music, two other baseline human activities' (14). There are obvious provocations here, such as what qualifies these particular practices as 'baseline' or more foundational than others, such as writing? Or again, why intuition is preferable to or different from discerning meaning? The process by which Thrift drafts this preferable taxonomy of forms and their values is not explained. Nor is what Thrift understands to fall under the genre of dance thoroughly outlined. Classical ballet, for example, a highly traditional, structured, routinised and exclusive practice, would more closely mirror the essay form than Thrift's description of dance, which seems to apply strictly to free-form improvisation.

While Thrift advocates for more affectively resonant genres, readers are not invited onto the dancefloor but instead remain within the critical essay genre for this particular argument. Thrift may explicitly argue for a shift to creative genres, to leave critical genres behind, but the focus in this book is a challenge to the critical genre and its received tenets via this very same method. Thrift argues that:

> [*Non-representational theory*] is a tentative book because it is not entirely clear what a politics of what happens might look like – indeed, given that so much of what I want to outline is avowedly experimental, perhaps too much in the way of clarity should not necessarily be counted as a good thing (although straightaway I can hear the criticisms from those who believe that theory should slide home like a bolt). (2)

Despite his avowed tentativeness, Thrift's unequivocal dismissal of existing social science methods does slide home like a bolt. He states that his argument is about adopting genres where judgement is not present; however, what he argues for, as we see in the previous quotation, is to make judgements and criticisms, and arguably without the engagement that is expected to underpin them. To practise critique is to take the risk of engaging closely and carefully with the logic of specific arguments. It involves the risk of owning a particular stand. Thrift does not offer a detailed analysis of how and why critique falls short. Thrift tries to be more creative and tentative with his *academic* writing and his actions highlight what he takes the markers of creative work to be. The implication (and surely it is one that adds the insult of artists to the injury of social scientists) is that creativity is less meticulous and precise than critical work, that creative practitioners express without forethought or intention, that they do not qualify or cite from history and tradition – in short, that all art is a rough sketch. In Thrift's argument, genres are ascribed essential identities that reduce their complex volatility, kinship and composition.

Deliberate Imprecision

This stated avoidance of clarity – a method based on the assumption that because life is constantly evolving we must remain tentative – is also a feature of John Law's influential *After Method: Mess in Social Science Research* (2004). In *The Affect Theory Reader* (2010), Melissa Gregg and Gregory J. Seigworth cite this book as 'a more than worthy and messy methodological text for what [they] have in mind' for a method following affect theory (25). According to Law, a key proponent of actor network theory, *After Method* is about 'what happens when social science tries to describe things that are complex, diffuse and messy' (2; see also Law and Hassard 1999). 'The answer', he argues, 'is that it tends to make a mess of it [. . .] because simple clear descriptions don't work if what they are describing is not itself very coherent' (2). Law advocates a shift away from clarity, claiming that: 'The very attempt to be clear simply increases the mess' (2). What Law might suggest here is that, ironically, presumably lucid social analysis is always already messy, the way we practise observation and representation complicate the sociality we participate in. Instead this desire for clarity is located as a problem that must be overcome by the pursuit of more suitable methods, messier ones, 'methods', Law argues, that are 'unusual to or unknown in social science' (2).

Outlining the scope of his endeavour, Law makes a strange delineation between social issues he believes can be quite aptly captured with existing social science methods and those that cannot. Interestingly, he suggests that there *are* some things that can be made clear and definite, and these include: 'income distributions, global CO_2 emissions, the boundaries of nation states' (2). Such delineation seems problematic, as one can easily think of numerous prominent examples where these things are at the very centre of ongoing contestation, such as the enduring Israeli-Palestinian Conflict, the ongoing Chinese occupation of Tibet, the Carbon Emissions Trading Tax and the Kyoto Protocol. Nevertheless, Law judges that 'these are the kinds of provisionally stable realities that social and natural science deal with more or less efficiently' (2).

In contrast to these supposedly straightforward 'realities', Law argues that there are things in the world with a different texture which these 'methods of academic inquiry don't really catch' (2). He makes a list of these differently textured things. They include: 'Pains and pleasures, hopes and horrors, intuitions and apprehensions, losses and redemptions, angels and demons, things that slip and slide, or appear and disappear, change shape or don't have much form at all [. . .]' (2). Law suggests that if these things *are* contained within 'our ethnographies, histories and statistics', it is because they have been 'distorted into clarity' (2). Law has faith that there *are* methods that will not distort social phenomena, but rather move with moving phenomena.

He locates a problem with knowledge at the root of the problem of method, namely our overinvestment in epistemology over ontology. Law sees the need for an important change, and as you can see in the following rationale, this is because he sees knowing to be something very different from feeling:

> If much of the world is vague, diffuse or unspecific, slippery, emotional, ephemeral, elusive or indistinct, changes like a kaleidoscope, or doesn't really have much of a pattern at all, then where does this leave social science? How might we catch some of the realities we are currently missing? Can we know them well? *Should* we know them? Is 'knowing' the metaphor we need? And if it isn't, then how might we relate to them? (2)

Law, like Thrift, proposes that, to be relevant, scholars need '*new ways*' (2), and encourages a move to 'embodied' and 'emotional' perspectives: 'Perhaps we need to know them through the hungers, tastes, discomforts, or pains of our bodies. [. . .] Perhaps we will need to know them through "private" emotions that open us up to worlds of sensibilities, passions, intuitions, fears and betrayals' (2–3). In this suggestion, we again see oppositions posited between the capacities of scientific and sensual methods, between knowing and being, between the mind and the body. Social science methods are set up as impersonal, impassive and disembodied. We might pause here and consider if this is a fair representation, for as Wolf Lepenies explains, as discussed in the first chapter, Auguste Comte, when creating sociology in its most positivist form, was driven by his obsessive love for the catholic novelist Clotilde de Vaux, as well as his own ascetic tendencies of hygiene (1988: 29). His sociological method – at once passionate and severe – was visceral, responsive and inextricable from his emotional and embodied life. It is possible to find mess within the seemingly neat histories and myriad applications of the methods we already use. But Law's argument does not seek to rattle assumptions about existing approaches, rather the focus is on new possibilities.

With social science methods ill-equipped to take on the 'maelstrom' of the material world, where are we to look for alternatives methods? Law explains that over the last two decades 'methods for the analysis of visual materials, performance approaches, and an understanding of methods as poetics or interventionary narrative' have been leading the way (3). Really setting social science up as last to the table, he notes that 'Market research, often more imaginative than academic social science, has developed methods such as tasting panels for understanding the non-cognitive and the ephemeral' (2). '[M]anagement consultancy', he adds, has also been innovative in its adoption of 'dramatisations, enactments and performances'. With the wider turn to creative methods, Law cautions, 'the world is on the move and social science more or less reluctantly follows' (2). Echoing Thrift's turn to the tentative, Law suggests that with these methods, 'knowing would become possible through techniques of deliberate imprecision' (3). Using this technique, Law argues that social scientists would thus allow for possibilities rather than stating a definitive point that will inevitably morph and shift. His book outlines exemplar studies that draw on different forms of metaphor, allegory, creative writing, performance and place-based research and oral storytelling. The examples are fascinating and most draw on traditional social science methods, primarily ethnography.

The introduction of new methods is not the issue here, but rather the caricature and dismissal of existing methods which is called upon to validate the need for the new. Thrift and Law argue for methods that can better convey complexity, but in the process actually represent methods to be less complex, contingent and entangled than they already are. As with Thrift's critical manifesto, there is nothing imprecise about Law's characterisation of traditional social science forms in his framing. They are set and ill-suited to a world of fluidity and affect. In a paradoxical claim that is both a didactic and definitive account of the world, Law contends that '[t]he world in general defies any attempt at overall orderly accounting' (6). Yet the desire to find a more accurate and precise method of accounting, albeit one that codes itself as open-to-anything, lies at the heart of Law's argument. The 'non-representational' is not, in practice, non-representational. Instead, it seeks only a *different* genre of representation. Ironically, while the method of deliberate imprecision is designed to help social scientists see the 'diffuse', the 'slippery', the 'indistinct' (Law 2004: 2), what we are offered by both Thrift and Law – in their focus on novelty – is a black-and-white picture of affective creativity on one side and static structural criticism on the other. The lack of clarity becomes exactly that – a loss of detail, of specificity and of all the intricacy and intersection that makes the social world, including humans' myriad attempts to represent it, a 'mess'.

Creative Writing as Dissent?

In response to this advocacy for creative practice as social science, some scholars have questioned the politics of framing creative outputs as acts of resistance, particularly as resistance to the rationalisation of the academy. Shifts in authorship may be hailed as an ethical act that offers the scholar a socially relevant and responsive practice, as Timothy Brennan explains 'the theorist as artist sees him or herself as being more political because s/he is involved in practice [. . .]

a term that appears to place [such scholars] in a more committed, hands-on role [...]' (2010: 278). Consonant with Thrift's argument for practice, various proponents of 'fictocriticism', for example, a method popular in anthropology that (as the name suggests) blurs fictive and academic writing, endorse creative and experimental forms as a challenge to institutional demands. Anna Gibbs captures this when she states that '[fictocriticism] is writing as research, stubbornly insisting on the necessity of a certain *process* in these days when writing is treated by those who determine what counts as research to be a transparent medium' (Gibbs 2005: 2). In these terms, Gibbs poses fictocriticism as a challenge to the fiscal ruthlessness of the contemporary research institution, or 'those who determine what counts'.

Michael Taussig (2010) similarly advocates fictocritical writing as a defence against institutional constraints. In Taussig's argument, the political camps, and their correlative genres, are starkly drawn. As an antagonist to 'Corn-Wolfing' (creative practice), Taussig posits 'agribusiness writing'. He asks, 'what chance is there for my anthropological project given the prevailing agribusiness approach to language and writing [...]?' (2010: 29). Taussig contends that 'agribusiness writing' is enforced in the university and alternatives censured. The 'prevailing approach' we might expect Taussig to be referring to here is a divestment in public universities, and in the humanities particularly. But instead he is concerned with a preference for criticism over experimental forms of writing: 'you can write about James Joyce, but not like James Joyce' (2010: 29). To 'counter the purported realism of agribusiness writing' (2010: 32), Taussig proposes counter-writing, 'the endorsement of the real as really made up' or the 'blurring of fiction and nonfiction ...' (2010: 33). In this argument, Taussig posits fictocriticism as an act of resistance to the academy's alleged attempts to censure creative research outputs. What results from his and other proposals for alternatives to critique is another possible act of censure.

It is suggested here that genre-blurring writing experiments pose a threat to the marketisation of the academy; however, the political outcomes of de-emphasising critical commentary in favour of 'practice' may not always aid dissent. Addressing the implications of fictocriticism's promotion of a creative turn, Brennan writes:

Overlooked here is the consonance of this approach with the plans of university administrators (Bard College is a well-known example) who wish to redefine the humanities by defunding inconvenient or 'useless' work of critical social theory in favour of the creative arts – a pattern equally evident in major fellowships in the humanities as well where the vast majority of grants go to artists (the Guggenheim, for instance). (2010: 297)

As Brennan notes, to relinquish judgement for play may enable, rather than prevent, the de-politicisation of the humanities. This is one of the issues at stake in the framing of the turn to creative outputs as an imperative for knowledge and ethics in general, rather than simply a challenge to social science's perceived conservatism or an extension of its methodological repertoire.

This oversight summons a point that political economist Wanda Vrasti raises about the affective turn more generally in her work on 'caring capitalism', namely the parallels between the celebration of creativity and autonomy and the current neoliberal celebration of creative entrepreneurism, which is, in reality, a celebration of the mass casualisation of the workforce. The dismissal of critique in favour of creative outputs is resonant with what Vrasti sees as the 'moral legitimating structures' that capitalism relies upon to 'make critique look ridiculous or exasperating' (Vrasti 2011: 1). Vrasti sees the 'valorization of affective and aesthetic competencies to compensate for the cutback in social services and safety provisions' as one of the current manoeuvres of neoliberal rhetoric, a shift that again parallels the turn from structuralist and demystifying methods to affect theory and 'experimentalism' (3). Embracing affect as the main social force, operating irrespective of structure, we are left with a scholarship that disables the function of critique to the point that it may inadvertently recuperate the rhetoric and action of the very political manoeuvres it aims to resist. Vrasti argues that affect is not a natural antagonist to neoliberalism, but one of the key forces of its reproduction (see also Illouz 2007; Berlant 2011; Gordon 2008). The trivialisation of critique and celebration of creative entrepreneurialism is arguably another. By pitting critical reflexivity against creative expression we limit our ability to notice and address such acts of co-option. The rush to claim intellectual contributions as novel, as heralding the next cutting-edge paradigm in social theory, could also be afforded the same scrutiny for how it fits with institutional pressures to record rapid progress and constant innovation (Chiew and Barnwell 2019). What we miss in this rush is a proper analysis of the socio-political determinants that frame which methods have value, and to whom, and at what times.

In sum, the above proposals champion the use of the creative and performing arts as an alternative to the inertia and authoritativeness of traditional social science forms. With non-representational theory, Thrift calls for a vocational practice, a craftsmanship, that he suggests is practical, participative and hands-on in expressing a non-subject-based experience. Law advocates methods that allow for change and shifts in definition and experience. In both proposals, a hierarchy between criticism and creativity is established. Traditional social science methods are set aside without a thorough (or sometimes even a cursory) explanation that shows *how* such projects miss their target. All this work is done in shorthand, and yet these are very bold claims: that social science is not already vocational, responsive, creative or even aware of the economic constraints on the production of intellectual work. Perhaps even more concerning than this, the premise that purportedly compels this shift – the demands of a changed social landscape – is also assumed rather than established. It is taken as given that critical or hermeneutic questions are the wrong ones for relating to affect or shifts in social atmospheres. In the sharp split between the value of ontology and epistemology, it is assumed that the lived concerns of everyday survival do not include questions about what determines the truth, or how we can access knowledge, or who has the power to decide what speech acts or decisions will be valid or verified. And yet, if we do look at the kinds of stories that creative practitioners are telling in the public sphere, these stark divisions between criticism and creativity, ontology and epistemology, and social and scholarly concerns are rather less distinct.

Paranoid Reading as Popular Reading

The method proposals discussed above suggest that if social scientists practise creative arts, if they make things like performances, films, short stories and so on, they are somehow positioned *within* the rich dynamics of the social world. Through these genres, scholars, it is claimed, can express the vitality of life in a way that cannot be achieved by scientific observation or critique because these forms objectify from outside. They distort mess into clarity, pinning life down like a butterfly on a board. In this book, I want to unsettle this polarised representation of genre. But it is also useful to consider that even if we accept this account of genres and agree that creative genres are the way forward, a few issues remain. If we actually look at what creative practitioners are expressing – this embodied and immanent truth social scientists have apparently been missing – what we find is that they are often engaged with the same themes as critics, namely paranoia, hermeneutics, questions about what constitutes the truth, who has access to the truth, how veneers are constructed, and so on. Thus the very themes that supposedly prove critique is an error, or suggest it is out of touch, that is its desire to demystify and focus on the construction of (false) consciousness, may also locate it as an expression of the same concerns that preoccupy the creative arts. So is critique then an immanent method? And were critics, with their eye to the unsaid, actually attuned to, if not carried along by, social currents all along?

When major literary critics note that the paranoid preoccupations within contemporary literature are emblematic of our age, they begin to muddy the notion that poststructural critique is behind the times and out of touch with concrete social matters because it is paranoid. Bemoaning Stephen King winning the National Book Award in 2003, Harold Bloom noted four living authors who he argued 'deserve our praise' – Thomas Pynchon, Phillip Roth, Don DeLillo and Cormac McCarthy (Bloom 2003). Which authors deserve our praise is obviously a point of conjecture, but Bloom gestures to the critical renown of the four writers here, three of which (Pynchon, Roth, DeLillo) overtly focus on the topic of paranoia and paranoid subjects. Writing for the *New York Review of Books*, Robert Towers (1988) pre-empted Bloom, when he described the new canon of postmodern writing as 'the paranoid school of American fiction' and hailed DeLillo as its 'chief shaman'. Contemporary with postmodern theory, these novels mark a point of resonance between theory and creative writing and position both as expressions of a paranoid zeitgeist.

Locating the paranoid style in post-Cold War creative genres, Aaron S. Rosenfeld (2004), argues that in the literature of the post-Cold War period, paranoia expanded to become a 'broad-based cultural pathology' (Rosenfeld 2004: 340). Where Sedgwick limits paranoid pathology to critique, Rosenfeld argues that 'plot' *generally* is 'a working through and out of a hermeneutic code' (359). That is the creation of a plot is always dependent upon the drawing of pre-emptive causal links. Fiction, following this, is not free of the para-noid style or representational anxiety. Novelists are directly engaged in asking questions about the representational and truth-telling limits or responsibilities of their practice and the codes of different genres. Devices such as unreliable narration and metafiction pose questions about verisimilitude, authorial presence and the line between fact and fiction. Novelists, in short, are engaged in questioning, rather than simply endorsing, the workings and affects of their representa-tional method, including its power to deceive.

Contrary to the idea that creative genres are less intentionally motivated and didactic, literary authors also use novels to make moral judgements about current political and intellectual debates. Discussing postmodern paranoid literature, Kathryn Hume (2000) argues that literature demands that we act *more* definitively than poststructural theory mandates. Here Hume suggests that these authors use their novels to make an argument about social affairs, not only to assert their own definitive viewpoint, but to suggest that, even in a postmodern world supposedly in flux and disarray, broader, socially defining points can and must be made:

> Postmodern theory may decentre the self to the point that no core remains that would permit agency, yet these writers stub-bornly commit themselves to the position that meaningful action must be taken. Mailer with his seven souls and Burroughs with his many alter egos literalise the notion that we may have become a congeries of selves, but they agree that some spark of awareness must make decisions and act. (2000: 439)

This purpose runs counter, for instance, to Thrift's idea that 'non-representational' or creative genres will allow social scientists 'to be resolutely anti-biographical and pre-individual, to trade in modes of

perception which are not subject-based' (2007: 7). For Hume, literature, even in its most experimental forms, can operate as a definitive
and didactic form of social commentary and critique which seeks
to know and name.

Taking this point further, Leo Bersani explores an example of the
novelist's social commentary in 'Pynchon, Paranoia, and Literature'
(1989). Writing about *Gravity's Rainbow*, Bersani explains that for
Pynchon what constitutes paranoia is the pinnacle question for our
age. This is a statement that problematises not only a dismissal of
paranoia as a fait accompli, but the suggestion that the creative arts
are the ultimate tool for a revolution *against* paranoia. Pynchon's
characterisation of literature also presents a provocative challenge
to the argument that creative genres are free from judgement and
ideology. Bersani explains that for Pynchon:

> [L]iterature, far from saving us from the controlling designs served
> by information systems, is itself an information system that threat-
> ens its readers' freedom by the very elusiveness of the demands
> which it makes on them [...] Literature is never merely an agent
> of resistance against networks of power-serving knowledge; rather
> it is one of that network's most seductive manifestations. It can
> never stand outside the oppressive manipulations of social reality
> and negate those manipulations by a willed alienation from history.
> (1989: 116)

For Pynchon, creative genres are not a refuge from structural
rationalisms, they are agential forces internal to them. Literature
is not an antidote to paranoia; it is itself concurrently productive
and symptomatic of the paranoid. As we know too well, art forms
have been used for propaganda, for instance agitprop by the Soviet
Union, precisely because they can work within semiotic and narrative conventions to solidify or coerce particular social sentiments.
Writers such as Margaret Atwood and Salman Rushdie have written about the political motivations of their fiction, as well as the
role of authors in the 'crisis of representation' (Mariani 1991; see
also Davis 1987).

Nor are suspicious themes limited to the American literary canon.
In popular culture more broadly, the desire for demystification is

clear, not only in theme but in method. The public interest in reading plots via a hermeneutics of suspicion suggests that faith in detection is not confined to social scientists. The protagonists of the most
popular genres of books, films and television programmes – crime,
legal dramas, even romantic comedies – engage in a sort of archae-
ology, following traces, uncovering secret injustices, pinpointing a
flaw in someone's psychology, or finding 'the one'. Through their
endeavours we vicariously sleuth and detect, attempting to collate a
verifiable chain of events or evidence a conclusion. Studies about the
rise of paranoid, conspiracy culture in the 1990s (concurrent with
affect theory) affirm this, citing the mass popularity of television programmes such as *The X-Files* (1993–2002; the show had a redux in
2016), with its pertinent tag-line: 'The truth is out there' (O'Donnell
2000; Melley 2000; Parish and Parker 2001; Knight 2002).

More recent television programmes have focused on hidden
truths in various ways. Prime-time programmes such as *Mad Men*
(2007–14), *Big Love* (2006–11), *Breaking Bad* (2008–13), *Homeland*
(2011–14) or *The Americans* (2013–18) focus on protagonists who
lead double lives and conceal secret identities. The charming Ad
Man, Don Draper, hides a past as the stolen valour veteran Dick
Whitman. The upstanding local businessman, Bill Henrickson, runs
for office in Salt Lake City, Utah hiding the fact he has three wives.
High-school science teacher, Walter White, conceals firstly the fact
he is dying of cancer and then his success as New Mexico's leading
crystal meth manufacturer from his family. War hero, Nicholas Brody,
an American marine held hostage in Iraq, secretly kneels down and
prays toward Mecca in his garage, and is suspected by the CIA to
have become a terrorist. Elizabeth and Philip Jennings, two soviet
KGB officers, pass as a suburban American couple – quickly duck-
ing into the garage at breakfast to violently interrogate an agent held
captive in their car trunk between serving the children orange juice
and cereal. In all of these stories we, the audience, are given a privi-
leged window into the truth. We share in the protagonists' anxiety
and empathise with their paranoia as they struggle to maintain a
coherent facade, or deconstruct one.

Secrets are revealed to us in yet more popular television programmes such as *In Treatment* (2008) and *The Sopranos* (1998–2007),
where we are privy to the intimate encounter between psychiatrist

and patient. In *True Blood* (2008), *Buffy* (1997–2003) and its spin-off *Angel* (1999–2004), *The Vampire Diaries* (2009) and two of the highest-selling book series of the twenty-first century, *The Twilight Saga* (2003–8) and *Harry Potter* (1997–2007), we are introduced to a world where the supernatural other walks among us, disguised as banal and human. Stieg Larsson's *Millennium Trilogy* and E. L. James's *Fifty Shades of Grey* series, two of the highest selling novel series in the past decade, also work with the idea of double lives and hidden plots. These creative renderings of social life represent a desire to look behind the veil to a truth which is revealed to us through dramatic irony – a view into someone's haunted dreams, their supernatural metamorphosis, their sexual proclivities or their clinical confessions – or at least to try to catch a glimpse of this activity.

These narratives give us the pleasure of indulging our suspicion, a fascination with what may be going on under the prosaic surface and an interest in the suppressed secrets or secret existence of others in our midst. But the ubiquity of dramatic irony in these shows also alludes to a desire to see the intricate workings of what it takes to construct or maintain a socially believable story or identity. We wish to see the truth, but also its progression toward, or dissonance with, social tell-ability. The prevalence of this narrative demonstrates that we, as a society, are interested not only in authenticity, but in its constitution. We are interested in watching representations and allegories about how life is lived (ontology and pragmatism), but importantly and specifically experiences which question knowledge, truth and representation (epistemology and veracity). Evidence that the public are still engrossed in the interplay of truth and representation is ubiquitous.

Forensic crime shows represent another recent trend in the truth-seeking genre, dominating prime-time television during the past decade. They celebrate our ability to make the invisible visible with science and technology. Interestingly, in a more recent development in this genre, the truth-seeking detective has become one who not only discerns a forensic truth but penetrates the world of the unknown: the forensic detective has given way to the psychic detective. Ann McGuire and David Buchbinder (2010) flag a trend in the 'psychic detective' genre of crime fiction. This rise in popularity coincides with the growing academic interest of affect theory, and mirrors its unique concerns about imperceptibility and the difficulty of applying forensic tools to spectral phenomena. But in the context of these narratives, this set of concerns can be read as next-level 'paranoid reading', as the detective pushes further and further into the unknown, always suspecting forces working from beyond. Television programmes, concurrent with the popularisation of affect theory, such as *Medium* (2005–11), *Supernatural* (2005–present), *The Mentalist* (2008–15), *A Gifted Man* (2011–12) and *The Ghost Whisperer* (2005–10), all feature detectives who solve crimes by psychically engaging with 'the other side', most often the deceased victims of crime. In the family drama *Six Feet Under* (2001–5) a family of funeral directors similarly converse with the spirits of their cadaverous clients. These narratives extend hermeneutics to intuiting the ineffable and human life to include posthuman agency.

McGuire and Buchbinder position this shift in the detective genre as a reasonable reaction to the current political climate, arguing that the rise of the psychic detective is symptomatic of post 9/11 trauma (2010: 293). McGuire and Buchbinder place these television programmes within the Gothic genre, or what Fredric Jameson calls 'its political-paranoid forms' (Jameson 1992: 290). Alluding to the American psyche, Jameson argues that sheltered socio-economic privilege acts as 'a protective wall through which you cannot see, and behind which therefore all kinds of envious forces may be imagined in the process of assembling, plotting, preparing to give assault' (Jameson 1992: 293). Just as the Cold War inspired creative works about paranoia and conspiracy, 9/11 brought the Gothic narrative to life: behind the spectacle of economic comfort, though uncannily within the borders of the nation, people were indeed plotting and preparing assault. Drawing from Jameson's metaphor, McGuire and Buchbinder argue that the interest in psychic detective narratives reflects a post-9/11 desire to gratify paranoid attention and to confront this perforated 'protective wall'.

McGuire and Buchbinder explain that this shift in the narrative of the genre is conceived as a shift in method. The transition from detective to psychic detective, they contend, was compelled by a decline of trust in traditional, ocular-based methods of forensic detection:

The events of 9/11 produced a complete paradox: the unseeable other had breached the boundaries of the nation state and left it metonymically in ruins. Yet the other remained invisible, even if agents could be seen and arrested. At the same time, however, the technologies of surveillance and visibility on which the nation had relied for its security and safety now became the mechanisms by which the citizens of the nation witnessed their betrayal, their exposure to danger and to fantasies of danger. In such a context, the traditional, the familiar forensic strategy – that is, a way of knowing the world and events – becomes manifestly inadequate. A new way of seeing, and therefore also of knowing, the world and events is required. (2010: 302)

Following this suspicion of the spectral, we are drawn to stories where we are made cognisant of what is unseen, private or secretive. We are given new faith with extra-sensory sight, the methods to reach beyond what is perceptible. The nature of the empirical, or of what seems stable and factual, was troubled by the events that led up to and followed the War on Terror. Trust in our ability to determine a causal chain of events, to predict or anticipate, was understandably shaken by the shock of the almost unbelievable televised event of planes hitting the Twin Towers on 9/11.

Thus while Thrift and Law argue that the rapid impetus of life gets lost in narration, particularly suspicious narratives, in this case hyper-vigilance is the creative response-in-motion to social change. The idea of detection as a means to navigate political insecurity finds a precedent in Walter Benjamin's analysis of the everyday experience of Parisian modernisation. 'In times of terror,' Benjamin states, 'when everyone is something of a conspirator, everybody will be in a situation where he has to play detective' (Benjamin 1983: 40). For Benjamin, detection is not averse to change, but an integral agent in both its momentum and acceptance. He suggests that the citizen 'develops forms of reaction that are in keeping with the pace of a big city [...] This is an indication of how the detective story, regardless of its sober calculations, also participates in fashioning the phantasmagoria of Parisian life' (41). McGuire and Buchbinder's argument can be read as an extension of Benjamin's: the specific form of detection that arises now is impelled by a specific form of terror. To *know* now we must penetrate the unseen, undetectable and unexplained agencies behind events.

Given the desire to infiltrate the unknown in popular culture, one could see the affective turn, with its focus on reaching seemingly imperceptible affect – which Massumi and Thrift define as an unrepresentable force (Massumi 1995; Thrift 2007) – as a direct expression of this wider turn to intuitive discernment. Psychic crime programmes challenge the idea of a truth that can be forensically revealed. In these shows the truth is located in the unknown, on the other side of perception, and can only be obtained by those with an extra-sensory gift, with an ability to 'cross over'. Importantly though, the method is still a relentless pursuit of truth, pushing *further* into the unknown in the search for answers, extending the bounds of the empirical world. In Massumi's influential argument (1995), the conception of reality is similar: affective, animating forces are beyond our perception, eluding our cognition and representations, and we need new methods to see or feel them. In sum, there is a focus on the unknown, on what is beyond the 'protective wall', which, in the case of an autonomous conception of affect, is the wall of human cognition.

What I am arguing here is that paranoid reading is widespread in popular reading, but the parallel goes further. Likened to the extension of forensic detection to psychic detection, the affective turn becomes an extension of, rather than antidote to, critique. It too pushes into paranoid territory, believing that we are being driven by forces we cannot see or access. It too seeks to transform inquiry based on a distrust of past methods that is prompted by current political uncertainties. Similar to the psychic detective, Massumi does not retreat from the possibility of understanding why we act. Rather, he argues that the locus of agency operates elsewhere and requires new methods of communication. Similarly shifting from the forensic and the spectral, affect theory calls for a kinetic mode of feeling as knowing. Hyper-paranoid, it anchors agency entirely outside our determination or control. The idea of an autonomous affect warns that the methods we trust to be emancipatory – the democratic rights to petition, information or speech – are ineffective because what motivates and animates life defies human agency, particularly language, criticism or causal reasoning. Read this way, the affective turn actively participates in and extends, rather than contradicts, a paranoid zeitgeist.

The fact that the scholars discussed do not acknowledge the continuing popularity of themes of secrecy, detection and imposture in public culture (let alone their own work) sits awkwardly alongside their claim to engage more generously with the beliefs, fetishes and common sense of everyday people. Latour and Sedgwick characterise critique as paranoid, or, in what is clearly and ironically a conspiracy metaphor, as an insidious malaise threatening scholars' ability to engage with social life. Sedgwick specifically calls critique 'paranoid reading' and uses metaphors of biological warfare to describe its pervasiveness (1997: 21). Latour, too, likens critique to the reasoning of conspiracy theorists and employs military metaphors in his argument (2004: 230–1). In 'After Suspicion' (2009), Felski argues that: 'Suspicion sustains and reproduces itself in a reflexive distrust of common knowledge and an emphasis on the chasm that separates scholarly and lay interpretation' (2009: 29). She argues that it is a method from which we must 'turn' if we are to 'build better bridges between theory and common sense, between academic criticism and ordinary reading' (31). In these arguments the hermeneutics of suspicion is cast as a negative mode of engagement, a tired and repetitive endeavour that has no relevance to the unpredictable fluidity of daily life.

However, if we do look towards the desires and beliefs of everyday people, to the stories of 'the popular' as the turn against critique wishes to do, then we see a dogged commitment to unveiling truths, to the idea that there is always more than meets the eye, and an assumption that truth *can* be found with relentless perseverance. Perhaps suspicion is not evidence of a gap between critical and common sense, as Felski argues, but rather evidence of their continuity. The repetition of paranoid themes across various genres of scholarship *and* high- and low-brow popular culture highlights a web of collective anxiety about how our lives are animated and authored.

To consider the turn to affect as congruent with social critique, summons a series of important and interconnected questions. For instance, if the new aim is simply another instantiation of a desire to give voice to the unseen or the silent present in social life, or to collate a complete image, does it really follow that a desire to demystify is no longer relevant? By characterising paranoia and a commitment to truth-seeking as synonymous with critique at the outset, the affective turn must ignore fascinating questions such as why is paranoia so pervasive? What motivates it? Why does it seem never to satisfy itself? Why, consistently, do we as a public sit and watch ourselves vicariously sleuthing secrets and cathartically confirming the fact that everyone is harbouring a hidden truth? Why are the most heralded and the most popular novels of our time peopled by paranoiacs who always turn out to be not so paranoid after all? Or as a correlative question aimed specifically at social science practice, why is it that we are constantly searching for new ways to capture a more authentic representation of social life? Why do we always have a sense that the truth of sociality eludes our efforts to describe it? What constitutes the affective vitality of paranoid methods? These questions are vital to a social – and sociological – hermeneutics of suspicion.

The popular culture examples discussed here, while selective, demonstrate that the anticipation and detection scholars like Thrift and Law hope to escape by shifting to the genres of the creative and performing arts is in fact already within these genres. This, I propose, is because we are not looking at two distinct generic registers – critical and creative – but at one, to draw on Law's term, 'mess'. Paranoid reading does not preclude the popular. Its epistemological questions do not exclude the lived ontology of social life, for sociality is not divided by these terms. Popular culture is enduringly interested in how truth is lived. No genre or author is immune to the influence of a political, social and historical milieu. All forms of storytelling are equally entangled in the matrix of social authorship. Literature and sociology, for example, are mutually involved in the processes of social inquiry and social definition. Similarly, paranoia is not the exclusive attribute of critical genres; driven by social and cultural determinants it is holistically integral to an engagement with sociality, or rather to sociality's engagement with itself. In addition to socio-political triggers like the Cold War and 9/11, the very act of creation or momentum inspires wariness as life constantly becomes fixed and unfixed. Identity, informed by the agency and experience not only of the self but of multifarious social agents and events, is at once anchored and fluctuating. It is this state, the need to respond and yet remain responsive in the knowledge that while you affect you are also being affected, that informs a quotidian suspicion: a suspicion that expresses itself in various social media, including critique, literature and on the silver screen.

Considering the fuller context of the methodological proposals for 'more affective' methods, it is evident that much of what is dismissed, such as suspicion, is actually crucial, even intensified, in grounding the very rationale of their intervention. We are right to be suspicious of the imposed coherence of arguments that hastily shuffle critique away and curious about the questions that continue to lurk behind their editorial dismissals. The division that Thrift and Law, for example, draw between creative and critical genres does not hold up because their characterisations of both sides of this polemic are unnecessarily reductive. They rob these diverse genres of their humility, their history, their ambidexterity and their interconnections. Creative genres, such as novels or poetry, do not provide an easy and hopeful counterweight to the cynical writing of the social sciences. As the juxtaposition of various genres illustrates, novelists, dramaturges and screenwriters grapple *alongside* social scientists with questions of representational credulity, ethics and authorship. Any attempt to tell a story is always already fraught with the question of its fidelity. In an attempt to build an interdisciplinary bridge between the methods of the social sciences, the humanities and the creative arts, the methodological proposals I discuss actually project chasms where there are shared questions and narrative motifs.

Proposing Alternatives

Thrift's 'non-representational theory' and Law's 'mess as method' share the premise that the social sciences are bogged down in the sceptical reading methods of critique and thus ill-equipped to face social and economic changes, be they everyday responses to events like 9/11 or the economic rationalisation of the academy. In the vein of Latour's 'Compositionist Manifesto' (2010), these social scientists offer creative expression as an antidote to critique. To remedy social science's apparently lagged response to affective events, Thrift and Law both argue that the social sciences must adopt research practices that eschew definitive claims, accommodate imprecision, reserve judgement and actively aim to experiment if they are to study affect or keep up with life's changes.

By accepting the notion that creative composition is inherently enabling, the architects of these alternative methods do not examine how genres are determined but rather promote particular genres. They do not open up the matter of how and why different styles are presumed to have divergent affective capacitates, or how forms produce varying social facts and feelings. In order to sustain an oppositional division between creativity and criticism, the characterisation of critical reading as essentially disabling is coupled with a representation of creativity as inherently liberating. In this context, genres associated with the creative and performing arts become strangely exempt from the political influence of Cold War suspicion and quotidian conspiracy that has infected the social sciences. Instead, genres selected as exclusively creative are represented as unencumbered, open channels for the dynamic forces of affect.

Thrift, in his 'non-representational theory', and Law, with his turn away from 'knowing', understand their interventions into social science methodology as novel departures from the desire to reveal the truth. However, as proposals purporting to *know* the right way to represent social life, their claim to have left a desire for epistemological mastery behind is unconvincing. Crucially, the polemic structure of their arguments limits their aims to consider the dynamics of social activity. The quite rigid characterisations of genres these manifestos develop, and also ascribe to past methods and present publics, do not allow for crossover or counter-intuition. Though framed as perceptive and flexible engagements with everyday life, the strict opposition between methods risks overlooking the nuances of how people often determine the laws of genre – their affects and truth-values – in real time.

The critique of critique is a twofold motion: it is a turn away from the suspicion of critical reading to the generativity of creative genres. As this and the preceding chapter argue, both actions are problematic and fall short of addressing their stated intention, which is to create a more generous academic practice, one which gives credence to the pragmatic power of beliefs, desires and the seemingly ineffable forces of affect – the how and why of what moves us. Paranoia seems to be the one feeling, sentiment, affect and/or emotion that holds no interest, relegated to a bygone age. Similarly, wedded to originary exclusions, what the argument ends up doing is denouncing the dogmatism of the critical method without engaging with the fact that this 'dogmatism' is vitalised by faith, a faith in the pursuit of truth or justice or the efficacy of counter-narration. Ironically, it is a faith that might serve as the perfect exemplar for how to work with the methods of the affective turn. As a 'matter of concern', the affect scholar might refrain, as Latour proposes, from calling critique out on its possible errors and assumptions, in short from disproving its facticity, in order to understand how it is formed by, and in turn forms, political reality. They might read it reparatively, as Sedgwick suggests, rather than through a paranoid diagnostic frame, which means drawing out how it is productive despite its arguable error. Following Massumi, they could pay attention to the affective flows that make critical writing compelling or stifling in various instances. However, the potential for such affective analysis risks being staunched by the very arguments that claim to define this potentiality. Instead, the social scientist's faith in the critical method's ability to unearth a truth is dismissed as old hat.

But despite the argument that such hermeneutic desires are no longer salient, the desire to locate the pinnacle of truth-telling practices, to discover the genre or form that will create the most authentic, responsive expression or representation of social life, still drives the methodologies discussed here. Reparative generosity remains a hope for this movement rather than a reality. To be 'reparative' the affective turn would have to become less paranoid about suspicion, to open up paranoia as a 'matter of concern', which it clearly is. In this light, we could begin to consider that the anticipation inherent to critical reading, but also to curiosity and creativity, is the very affective force that drives this turn and the broader sociality of which it is an expression.

4

Ordinary Paranoia

Over the past decade there has been a growing chorus of discontent with what are perceived to be the suspicious reflexes of critical methods. The common charge is that critique has become paranoid and stagnant, unable – and often unwilling – to register the dynamic attachments and affects that vitalise everyday life. My aim here is to unsettle the seemingly disparate identities that justify this turn – the critical, structural forms of attention assigned to the critic on one side and the affective, dynamic attentions that animate everyday life on the other. To open up the lived and creative dynamics of suspicious attention, the affects of critique, this chapter addresses an intriguing, internal conflict within a text that has been widely commended for its response to calls for methodological change, Kathleen Stewart's *Ordinary Affects* (2007). Though it is marked as a departure from 'paranoid reading', I argue that Stewart's work gives us reason to reconsider the potential, character and social utility of suspicious attention, and thus the division of critical and social methods. By highlighting this counter-narrative within Stewart's work, my discussion also addresses broader questions about the nature of affect and the value of critical reading that have arisen in recent and prominent debates about methodology.

In consonance with Stewart, I am in favour of inclusive forms of inquiry that consider non-human-centred modes of change and agency. However, I envision that this approach would mean not excluding a range of methods and possibilities from the outset. With this in mind, instead of asking how critique could be more than suspicious, with the hope of forging a new method, I want to ask a slightly different question, namely how might this suspicion be more than critique? And by 'more than' I mean how might the desire to reveal hidden motives and agencies have a broader social location and purpose? How might it resonate in and with logics that blur what are presumed to be the distinct realms of critical and common thought? In this frame, we have the potential to decentre critical hermeneutics in a way that does not seek to exclude or dismiss it as erroneous or obsolete, but rather considers the way that all methods – not just a select 'better' few – are immanent to the social affective spaces they engage.

As Ben Anderson notes in *Encountering Affect* (2014), 'there is now an extraordinary proliferation of versions of what affect is and does' (7). He explains that this is because an interest in affect orients 'inquiry to life and living in all its richness' (7). However, critical voices within affect theory have variously argued that certain questions about living, namely critical questions about identity politics and structural inequalities, have sometimes been set aside unnecessarily (Hemmings 2005; Thien 2005). Anderson aims to address the conflict between critique and affect by offering 'a specific practice of critique [that] can sit alongside and compliment speculation and description as ways of relating to affective life' (19). With my close reading of Stewart's ethnography I hope to show that we could also face this conflict by considering how existing forms of critical attention, in all their suspiciousness, might already be viable methods for navigating social shifts. My argument therefore joins efforts to diversify the methods we can use to engage with affect by addressing key theoretical and methodological tensions within the field. It raises questions about how we ascribe values and affects to particular modes of analysis and re-enlists critical hermeneutics, via Stewart, as a creative, dynamic social method.

A Provocative Paradox

Stewart has been portrayed as one of the primary advocates of 'non-representation' and 'creative experimentation' (Blackman and Venn 2010: 13), and *Ordinary Affects* as one of the 'most widely circulated books on affect' (Frank and Wilson 2012: 873). In *Ordinary Affects'* 115 autobiographical fragments – the longest stretching across five pages, the shortest just four lines – Stewart narrates scenes from her everyday life where people she knows, meets or sees respond to as yet undefinable, affecting forces. The fragments are prefaced by a short, critical introduction that positions *Ordinary Affects* as a correction to critical, structural and representational forms of social science and, in realisation of the current methodological directive, as an intuited and creative rendering of everyday life. In the very first sentences, Stewart aligns her study with the aims and terminology that codify the intervention described above. '*Ordinary Affects* is an experiment, not a judgment,' she argues, '[c]ommitted not to demystification and uncovered truths that support a well-known picture of the world, but rather to speculation, curiosity and the concrete [. . .]' (Stewart 2007: 1).

The ethnography can be read as a realisation of the proposals for methodological change cited in my introduction. In the opening pages of *Ordinary Affects*, and in a series of related articles, Stewart draws inspiration from the turn against critique's key theorists. In 'Weak Theory in an Unfinished World' (2008), for instance, Stewart cites Sedgwick's arguments against paranoid reading as an impetus for her work (72; see also 2011). In 'Atmospheric Attunements' (2010), Stewart also names Thrift and Latour as inspiration for her 'writing and thinking experiment' (Stewart 2010: 445). 'Following these tendencies to rethink theory and writing,' she explains, 'my point here is not to expose anything but to pencil in the outline of what Thrift (2007) calls a geography of what happens: a speculative topography of everyday sensibilities [. . .]' (Stewart 2010: 445). Noting precedents for *Ordinary Affects*, Stewart also praises fictocriticism's blurring of fact and fiction, which, marked as more sensorial than critical prose, 'leaves the reader with an embodied sense of the world' (2007: 6).

Stewart represents affect as unresponsive to structural, analytic and critical methods. Such methods, she contends, cannot capture the affective dynamics of everyday life. According to Stewart, traditional '[m]odels of thinking slide over the live surface of difference at work in the ordinary to bottom line arguments about "bigger" structures and underlying causes' and 'obscure the ways in which a reeling present is composed out of heterogeneous and non-coherent singularities' (4). Affects, she argues, 'are not the kind of analytic object that can be laid out on a single, static plane of analysis' (3). Echoing Massumi's arguments about the stagnating effects of representation and critique, Stewart also explains that her work 'tries to slow the quick jump to representational thinking and evaluative critique long enough to find ways of approaching the complex and uncertain objects that fascinate because they literally hit us or exert a pull on us' (4). To avoid categorising affects or trying to determine their cause or identity, Stewart employs stylistic techniques that, on the one hand, forestall a definitive description of affects, but on the other hand, determine affect as naturally indeterminate. Most notably, affect, in her descriptions, is tentative and unclassified, referred to only as 'something': 'An opening onto *something*' (2007: 72); 'a something waiting to happen' (72); 'things throw themselves together into something that feels like *some*thing' (76); '*Everyone* knew that something was happening, that they were *in* something' (79).

After shedding the static and paranoid impositions of structure and critique, Stewart, we might assume, is set to reveal an unsuspicious and uncritical public. However, what we find in *Ordinary Affects*, contrary to the arguments of some of its cited influences, is a collective commitment to anticipatory reading and causal sense-making as methods, not just of scholarship, but of survival. Stewart's introduction reinforces the claim that a hermeneutics of suspicion has lost its everyday purchase; however, in stark contrast, her ethnographic fragments present an unmistakeably hyper-vigilant public.

Stewart's fragments are populated by the characters and settings we might expect to find in the postmodern paranoia novels of Thomas Pynchon or the offbeat Americana of David Lynch's television miniseries *Twin Peaks*. In North American trailer parks and strip malls, citizens are vigilant and reactive. *Ordinary Affects*' 'atmosphere is', as Ben Highmore notes, 'simultaneously small-town gothic, blue-collar naturalism, and main-stream surrealism' (2011: 8). Stewart includes social anxieties about day-care centres and ritual abuse (2007: 64), the moral panic of teenage massacres (74), impending Christian apocalypses (108), mysterious illnesses (43), border anxiety (123–4), 9/11 (121, 124) and public surveillance (82). Trailer park eccentrics and citizens fight, or fail to fight, the chemical companies whose covered-up contamination of the water supply is responsible for their ailments (28, 84, 33, 91). Disgruntled young men, in forgotten, post-industrial cities, turn to neo-Nazism, wanting someone to blame (56). People are addicted to poker-machines (72, 95), wonder drugs (75) and wander around in shopping centres aimlessly looking to fulfil a mysterious desire (61). With strikingly symmetrical irony then, Stewart's critical framework, which draws from Sedgwick's argument that paranoid reading is a tired, ivory-tower method (Stewart 2008: 72) and gestures away from concerns about cause and underlying agencies (2007: 4), is challenged by her own commitment to documenting the ongoing ubiquity and gravitas of suspicious reading in everyday life.

Stewart's ethnography can be read as a realisation of the methodological calls described in the opening of this essay. However, I argue that its paradoxes also challenge the redundancy of the hermeneutics of suspicion – as a common, interpretive method – in a world where authorial agency is radically distributed, and yet individual culpability remains an immediate concern. In this social context, people may be privy to the social and economic dynamics that filter their choices but must at the same time contend with powers – for example, credit and insurance companies – that increasingly hold them individually accountable for risk and action. Drawing out this tension, my reading locates suspicion as a living, dynamic form of attention, at the heart of Stewart's ethnography. I argue that if we recognise, rather than dismiss, the vitality of suspicion, we can begin to unravel why wariness is such an untiring form of attention in scholarship *and* within the wider rhythms of social life. Breaking from an essentialist reading of the hermeneutics of suspicion as an inert and uncreative method, we can consider how 'paranoid reading' might already be a feasible way to deal with the shifting ambiguities of our mercurial social structures and the authorial agencies they involve.

Ordinary Paranoia

The world Stewart creates in her fragments compels us to ask whether paranoid methodologies are *obscuring* the true voice of the social, or if the paranoia of critical methodologies is a manifestation of a broader, social atmosphere. To readers, an internal conflict becomes evident. Stewart aligns her position with Sedgwick's characterisation of paranoid reading as an outdated methodology. However, what we see consistently and persuasively in the ethnographic fragments of *Ordinary Affects* is that paranoia is a vital, orienting method in the social milieu Stewart represents. Reading experiences of suspicion in this context also lends a different texture to structure, readability and wariness than the broader turn from critique – and Stewart's introduction – puts in place. Drawn directly from Stewart's post-9/11 North American context, a setting of immediate political, ideological and economic unrest, these characters – call-centre employees, neofascists and retirees alike – sense momentums that 'threaten' to gather or disperse, unhinging their lives in banal and dramatic ways. In the environment Stewart studies, it is not the imposition and rigidity of structure that causes a sense of unease among publics, but the *volatility* of such determinants.

Despite initial positioning against structural concerns, Stewart's ethnography is consonant with a current resurgence of sociological interest in how demographics emerge or change in response to economic crises (Neilson and Rossiter 2008; Hardt and Negri 2009; de Peuter 2011; Standing 2011a). Guy Standing, an economist and public intellectual, signals an emerging class called the 'precariat', a heterogeneous demographic united by their perpetual state of economic insecurity. It is a global class, Standing argues, that feels: 'Everything is fleeting' (2011b). For Standing this is a feeling that can be anchored in processes such as the casualisation of the workforce. The demographic Standing argues for, the 'precariat', resonates with the 'emergent' class that Stewart describes in *Ordinary Affects*. The ethnography is awash with citizens who are wary of widespread financial instability, who are living in a permanent state of simmering unease. In a fragment called 'short circuit', for example, Stewart articulates the affective toll of industrial dispute, risk and uncertainty, an anxiety that defines the 'precariat':

> [H]er brother makes foreman at GE after twenty some years on the line [. . .] There's a strike over healthcare cuts and job security. He and the other foreman have to cross the picket line. It's horrible. He's been a union steward. He's given union speeches. Now things are getting ugly. Something powerful and painful flashes through him. (2007: 14–15)

Though Stewart marks affect as 'something' here, the flash is readable as the lived struggle of structure. The foreman has a sense of

solidarity with his fellow workers, but is threatened by the obliga-
tion of his new role and the living it provides him. The workers'
rights erode before his eyes as the workforce becomes more 'flexible'. His affective experience is a profoundly sociological one. It
is the feeling of being implicated and systemic, complicit in what
grips you. As Judith Butler states in her work on global ethics:
'Precarity exposes our sociality, the fragile and necessary dimensions of our interdependency' (2012: 148). In this pithy description,
Butler presents precarity as a condition that emphasises our citizenship in a broader social economy or ecology. Butler describes this
experience as the response to contemporary fiscal-crisis, and it is
this economically unstable world Stewart documents in *Ordinary
Affects*. Edging her vision closer to sociological commentaries about
the impact of economic instability than she acknowledges, Stewart's
fragments offer a description that unsettles the division between '
"bigger" structures' and fluid, everyday affects set out in her critical
introduction (4).

The stories in *Ordinary Affects* speak to discourses other than the
desire to revolutionise method. Indeed they can be read as a compelling case for the quotidian value of suspicious reading. Delving into
Stewart's previous *oeuvre* reveals quite a stated fascination with the
cultural importance of paranoia in contemporary US culture (1999,
2000; with Harding 1999, 2003). In *Paranoia within Reason*, Stewart's
essay, 'Conspiracy Theory's Worlds' (1999), for instance, places her
research within a body of work that recognises conspiracy culture
as more than just a hangover from Cold War McCarthyism. In these
essays, suspicious feelings are located at the heart of ongoing political problems. Douglas R. Holmes's 'Tactical Thuggery: National
Socialism in the East End of London' (1999), for example, gives an
insight into how the British National Party has used rhetoric conflating the decline of the welfare state with incoming migration, in
a deliberate manoeuvre to breed nationalist and racist paranoia. Ten
years beyond the publication of this article, and exacerbated by the
instability surrounding the global financial crisis, this same sentiment was seen in the BNP's dubious attempts to explain the 2011
riots on the streets of London. Stewart's inclusion in this volume
positions her within a discourse that sees paranoia – and specifically
the productive, everyday force of paranoid reading methods – as

a topic worthy of ongoing analysis. Here, paranoia is outlined as a common structure of thought, a schema for how knowledge is collated and then acted upon in everyday scenarios. The prevalence and risks of pattern-reading, in this context, begin to signal a more general act of interpreting and inferring causality.

Though intended as a departure from paranoid narratives, the fragment form Stewart adopts in *Ordinary Affects* also encourages a meditation upon causal and relational forms of deduction.[1] The fragment structure derives from the pottery shard or the torn papyrus: the irresolvable, incomplete archaeological form. In *The Fragment: An Incomplete History*, Glenn W. Most suggests that: 'Precisely by being incomplete, [the fragment] stimulates our imagination to try and complete it, and we end up admiring the creativity that would otherwise have languished within us' (Most, in Tronzo 2009: 12). A collection of splinters works as an asyndeton, encouraging the reader to engage in a hermeneutic reading method, anticipating and assuming that what constitutes the whole can be read in a part, or even an omission. The fragment form operates within a frame of causality. We read patterns, make deductions about their relation and the arrangement of agency within them. Thus while Stewart's fragments aim to work against a sense of totality (2007: 1), Stewart also relies on the connective inferences of pattern recognition to weave *Ordinary Affects* moments into a zeitgeist.

Suspicion drives knowledge; it is the knitting together of seemingly disparate events and utterances into a pattern that can be read and responded to. It serves the desire for meaning and explanatory

---

[1] The fragment form has a strong history as an academic genre. Examples include Jacques Derrida's *The Postcard: From Socrates to Freud and Beyond* (1987), Theodor Adorno's *Minima Moralia: Reflections from a Damaged Life* ([1951] 2005) and Marcus Aurelius' *Meditations* ([1558] 1998). According to Jacqueline Lichtenstein: 'The fragment can be linked to the literary tradition, that of the *formes brèves* (short literary forms) favoured by French moralists of the seventeenth century (2009: 125). Including: 'La Rochefocauld's *Maximes*, La Bruyère's *Caractères*, Pascal's *Pensées* and – the earliest of these – Montaigne's *Essais*' (Lichtenstein, in Tronzo 2009: 125). Drawing from literary precedents as Stewart does, Gertrude Stein's *Tender Buttons* (1914) also warrants mention. Lichtenstein asks us to note that 'all these titles are plural nouns' (2009: 125). *Ordinary Affects* would fit this tradition.

logic that Stewart, following Barthes, pushes into the background, but nonetheless pursues *and* provokes. It is not as though causality or meaning are imposed structures that, when miraculously removed, will reveal a public undesirous of meaning and justification. Processes of relation and deduction are integral to thinking and creating and living. It is precisely these ever-evolving patterns of causality that drive *and* test the people of *Ordinary Affects*.

The scenes that Stewart recounts in her ethnography affirm the ordinariness, the commonplace nature, of the hermeneutics of suspicion as a methodology for relational living. They create a picture of American life where people are permanently attuned to the threat of mysterious 'somethings' threatening to 'throw themselves together'. The individual suffers an anxiety of influence, grappling with the social authorship, or the radically distributed agency, of life. Capturing the tone of the book, as well as creating a point of origin, Stewart begins her first fragment 'Dog Days' with the ominous line 'It's been years now since we've been watching' (10). 'Something surges into view like a snapped live wire', it is both 'real' and 'delusional' (9). 'The dogs take to sleeping in nervous fits and starts' and 'cower under legs for no good reason' (9). They 'whimper at the sound of branches brushing up against the bathroom window in the still of the night' (9). The dogs are attuned to some mysterious threat, but then just as easily snap out of it and resume their tail-wagging play. In this fragment we are introduced to the kind of world Massumi describes in 'The Autonomy of Affect' (1995), where forces surge beneath our human perceptions, affecting our everyday lives. However, as we can see, this is not a world devoid of scrutiny, as a turn away from critique might assume. Rather, the autonomy of affect creates perfect conditions for suspicion. The subject remains ever alert to an unseen presence – their agency is always already thwarted in the face of a power that they allegedly cannot name or even perceive.

Thus, despite a series of proposals from scholars such as Latour, Sedgwick and Massumi that insist everyday life is no longer animated by a desire to determine the true cause of events, and that affect is impervious to such attention, in *Ordinary Affects* we finally arrive at an illustration of this much-invoked 'ordinary' only to discover that the indeterminacy of affect *fuels* paranoid reading. Stewart introduces us to a milieu where people cannot define exactly what forces are at work but nonetheless always have an inkling that 'things are happening' (2007: 21). The vigilant attention that is introduced in the first line is repeated again and again throughout the book. In the very next fragment 'Attention is distracted, pulled away from itself. But the constant pulling also makes it wakeful, "at attention"' (10). This guarded motif is one of the most prevalent in the book:

And the habit of watching for something to happen will grow (12)

There's a politics to ways of watching and waiting for something to happen (16)

It's the paying attention that matters – a kind of attention immersed in the forms of the ordinary but noticing things too (27)

Watching and waiting has become a sensory habit . . . Hypervigilance has taken root (35)

[Rogue intensities] incite . . . the most ordinary forms of watchfulness (45)

It's like flexing one's watching and waiting muscles, keeping them limber [. . .] Not exactly 'passive', it's hypervigilant (50)

Forms of attention and attachment keep [the self] moving: the hyper-vigilance . . . the vaguely felt promise that something is happening, the constant half-searching for an escape route (58)

As the repetition of this motif demonstrates, vigilance is intrinsic to Stewart's representation of everyday life. This 'Watchfulness' (45), linking the anticipation of others and Stewart's own ethnographic 'gaze', works against the presumed split between academic and quotidian concerns that frames the book to draw the hermeneutics of suspicion – and the hermeneutics vital to simply *living* – into alignment.

As argued in the previous chapter, the proposed methods of the affective turn – to be attuned and attentive to the emergent, to follow things where they lead without judgement or scepticism – seem to resonate with paranoid forms of attention. We can see this parallel become explicit in a fragment where Stewart recalls a former neighbour who filmed his daily life. One night, he gives Stewart and several other anthropologists a video of himself breathing heavily as he walks through the woods. Stewart reflects on the mode of attention in the film, where causality is not past but rather anticipated in the present:

> Things are (potentially) happening and he is in the habit of paying strict attention. But he is not necessarily in the habit of getting to the bottom of things or of making a decision or a judgment about what to do. He is making a record of his own ordinary attention to things and it's this – the record of his attention – that he shares indiscriminately with the anthropologists gathered next door [. . .] (36)

In reference to this man's methodology, Stewart explains that: 'He's an extremist, pushing things for some reason, but the close, recorded attention to what happens and to the intense materiality of things make some kind of sense to a lot of people [. . .]' (36). Stewart reads this man's film as a shift toward attention without 'judgement' or discrimination, a shift in which the author is merely a watchful channel. It is a method, she notes, that isn't so different from her own. At this point, Stewart's argument begins to truly twist back upon itself. It becomes difficult, when she so explicitly considers the potential utility and sense of hyper-vigilance, to reconcile her project with its critical framework, namely her subscription to the arguments of Sedgwick and Latour. Latour derides critique because he suggests that it is beginning to resemble conspiracy theory. However, in Stewart's text, the anthropologist, like the man with the video camera, remains permanently attuned to their surroundings, even in the most innocuous circumstances.

Stewart does not break from paranoid logic; she effectively locates herself in a circle of constant watchfulness. Often engrossed in hyper-paranoid milieus, she watches – indeed joins with – those who are watching and waiting for 'something' to happen. In this context, the idea that affect, as a radically dispersed and unrecognisable non-human agency, is governing our actions and events does not quell or suspend suspicious attention. It does not dampen the desire to pre-empt and anticipate. Rather, hyper-vigilance, as a form of responsive attention, is actually exacerbated by the notion that agencies beyond our control can arise from anywhere at any time. *Ordinary Affects* is a noted exemplification of the affective turn's method proposals, and yet a pejorative description of paranoia unravels in the ethnography.

It is precisely this paradox that marks *Ordinary Affects* as a motivating point from which to refocus the current desire to adequately represent what motivates and matters to people, and to re-gauge suspicion's salience to this practice.

The Social Rhythm of Suspicion

Ordinary Affects, despite its affiliation with Thrift's theory, is not an example of 'non-representation'. Indeed, its theme fits neatly with received notions of paranoia, like the delusions of people fretting over alien experimentation or fluoride in the water supply. Leo Bersani suggests that stereotypical iterations of paranoia are 'used as if it were merely synonymous with something like unfounded suspicions about a hostile environment' (1989: 99). Stewart comes close to offering us this tropological paranoia, with all the requisite ingredients, yet by affirming the ordinariness of this affect at other turns, the characters which populate *Ordinary Affects* point to 'something' that is a little more ambiguous.

Stewart participates in the turn against critique, framing social sciences' critical methodologies as 'unhelpful'. However, in spite of its posturing, one *could* read *Ordinary Affects* as an account of how suspicion is not a malaise or threatening attack that must be fought off or from which people need to be saved. Instead, paranoia gives a tenable rhythm to people's lives. It has a counter-intuitive, even positive momentum that creates coherent identities and communities. In *Ordinary Affects*, the sense that something is always slightly off-beat unites people as often as it divides them.

In the fragment 'Being in Public,' for instance, sociality is ultimately anchored in a shared suspicion. Stewart writes that, in public: 'There are hard lines of connection and disconnection and lighter, momentary affinities and differences' (42). To exemplify this, she lists ways that people simultaneously differentiate themselves from and align themselves with social groups:

> Little worlds proliferate around everything and anything at all: mall culture, car culture, subway culture, TV culture, shopping culture, all teams and clubs and organisations [...] addictions of all kinds [...] diseases of all kinds, crimes, grief of all kinds, mistakes, wacky ideas. (42)

Then in the fragment's closing line, to gather together her lists, Stewart offers a final drawstring: 'But everyone knows there's something not quite right' (42). This fragment can be read as working against the idea that suspicion is fractious. It posits a suspicious inkling as the common thread that unites 'everyone' – be they in the 'country club' or the 'sex group' (42). Similarly, in 'The "We" of Mainstream Banality' people are united in their mutual belief in government conspiracies, importantly in a light-hearted way, adorning their cars with bumper stickers, like the playfully homonymic 'Bush bin Lyin' (28). In both these fragments, people create identities and communities through shared suspicion. In creating a 'Them' they also create an 'Us'.

In this case, paranoia is not simply a delusional social malaise or 'an unfounded suspicion about a hostile environment' (Bersani 1989: 98); it is an effective mechanism with which to navigate the real-time revision of social orders. Indeed, paranoia emerges to be, as Marita Sturken describes in her work on contemporary culture, 'a social practice' 'rather than a pathology' and 'an integral aspect of the ways in which citizens mediate their relationship to political power' (1997: 77). The ubiquitous sense of suspicion is a constant reminder that the foundational narratives of our lives are precariously positioned due to constant shifts in the agential arrangement of social authorship. *Ordinary Affects*, read this way, compels us to consider not how 'unhelpful' the scholarly desire to know and name is, but how alike it is to our everyday desire to be part of 'something' recognisable or to give an authentic account of ourselves to others – to know where we stand.

Stewart does not acknowledge this paradox between the condemnation of a 'hermeneutics of suspicion' as an irrelevant discourse and the affirmation of hyper-vigilance as a pervasive form of social attention as it runs through her body of work. Is this because she sees the paranoia of academic reading as separate from the hyper-vigilance of the everyday people she writes about? This separation – and it also operates within other arguments against critique – seems to assume that when everyday people are compelled by something they perceive to be operating beneath the surface they gesture to affect, whereas if a scholar has the same experience, if they read a text and are unsettled and instructed by something lurking within it, 'something' that is not self-evident but somehow present and potentially volatile, then, to draw on Latour's diagnosis, they are a savage iconoclast (2004). However, in *Ordinary Affects*, this division cannot be sustained.

Stewart is magnetised, as the endurance of her work on paranoid culture attests, to the vigilant, interpretive attention that is also her own. Writing is *of* life. As the physicist Niels Bohr noted: 'We are part of this nature that we seek to understand' (in Barad 2007: 26). Though this connection languishes in *Ordinary Affects*, the unity of professionals and publics pursuing hidden agencies can be seen nonetheless. Latour, Sedgwick and Stewart argue that paranoid frames are out of touch with social imperatives, but it is the stylistic correlations between their own arguments, their own 'conspiracist' motifs, that point to the ubiquity and obvious relevance of practices of scepticism, wariness and de-mystification in everyday life.

Latour's and Sedgwick's characterisations of critique as a virulent and insidious malaise lines up perfectly with Stewart's suspicious citizens, who see veiled threats emerging everywhere, from the supermarket to their neighbour's lawns. For Latour, critique has fallen into the hands of 'conspiracy theorists' like 'weapons smuggled through a fuzzy border to the wrong party'; it 'disarmed once matters of fact', 'eat[ing them] up [with] the same debunking impetus', resulting in a 'sort of darkness' 'fall[ing] on campuses' (2004: 232). For Sedgwick critique threatens 'if it persists unquestioned, [to] unintentionally impoverish the gene pool of literary-critical perspectives and skills' (1997: 21). These malignant characterisations are so like the fears of the characters in *Ordinary Affects* that, when reading these proposals, readers cannot help but see the parallels between the concerns of scholarship and the concerns of everyday citizens.

Thus *Ordinary Affects* leaves us questioning just why these sleuthing methods seem to be so entrenched, so omnipresent, not just in academic methodologies but in popular culture, in our everyday dealings with people and in our very economic system: a market that feeds on confidence but also rumour and fear. Why is suspicion's hold so powerful that even those who claim to violently break from it are still entranced? The affective turn's warfare metaphors and the political imperatives of their arguments are themselves driven by the suspicion that their own 'matters of concern' are under threat. In the struggle over authorial agency that lies at the heart of paranoia, Spinoza's process of being concomitantly affected and affective is clearly illustrated ([1677] 2001). This state of scrutiny centres on the very anxiety between what is self and what is other, between what is a compulsion or a choice, or who is authoring and how. Paranoia is a process dedicated to speculation, to cartography, to taking itself and others apart to see how they work. Such suspicion is an unrelenting, vital process that never seems to reach the closure it desires, but continues to desire it nonetheless. It expects change, and braces for the resonating effect a tremor might initiate in the social fabric.

Thus, rather than being a method to dismiss, suspicion seems to be precisely the place to look if we are to understand the nature of social organisation and how it is responsive to itself. By fore-fronting the practices of reading patterns and inferring authorial agencies, we can begin to consider structure, not as something static to be attenuated by altruism and creativity, but rather as a fluid process of structuration where people must navigate life even as its coordinates shift.

'Creative Paranoia': A Social Method

Reading Stewart's *Ordinary Affects* alongside Lauren Berlant's *Cruel Optimism* (2011), which she cites as an influence, clarifies Stewart's experiment and lends insight into how the experience of everyday suspicion is textured. Berlant's text has similar themes, but differs from Stewart's in style. Though it also deals with social experiences of contingent presents and projective fantasies, Berlant tries to locate them with existing attempts to chart how people live in particular affective landscapes, such as Marxist and queer theory or the sociology of everyday life. Berlant carves out a slightly different critical space to Stewart, but it is one where Stewart's work can be read, with critical reparation, in light of different kinships. In this context, what Stewart has to say about paranoia, as a social atmosphere, becomes a constructive dialogue with, rather than a subscription to, 'the affective turn'.

Importantly, Berlant picks up on the same tenor of hyper-vigilance that Stewart documents and marks it as a key theme of modern citizenship. Berlant clarifies that her work 'focuses on dynamic relations of hypervigilance, unreliable agency, and dissipated subjectivity under contemporary capitalism' (2011: 9). In Berlant's text, as in Stewart's, being vigilant is how people feasibly deal with the turbulence of political, economic and social climates. Individuals try to be alert to how their attention is constantly being diverted toward spectres of prosperity, whether it is in the orchestrated detours of shopping malls or the wish-fulfilling images of advertising. Hyper-vigilance escalates as people 'get wise' to the emptiness or endless deferral of such promises. Exploring citizen's everyday response to contested agencies, these texts make a markedly different argument to the affective turn with which they are associated. Here, the pragmatic approach to social change that the affective turn is so eager to create is already apparent in everyday citizens' shrewd incredulity, their guarded attempt not to be duped and to stay afloat amid social unease.

To be vigilant, in *Cruel Optimism*, is not to be delusional. Instead, you *need* to read the present with a tentative wariness if you are to keep up with society's structural indeterminacy. The shifting nature of social currents and the conflicting perspectives that interpret and reinterpret these shifts in real time demand that people be 'anticipatory', one of the key markers of 'paranoid reading' (Sedgwick 1997: 9). 'If the present is not at first an object but a mediated affect,' Berlant explains, 'it is also a thing that is sensed and under constant revision, a temporal genre whose conventions emerge from the personal and public filtering of the situations and events that are happening in an extended now whose very parameters (when did "the present" begin?) are also always there for debate' (2011: 4). In the reality Berlant describes, people live tentatively. But they must also make decisions and take actions even though they cannot always control the consequences or even the original terms by which these decisions are made. The conventions of life's genres, its structural determinants, are socially authored in the very acts of living and interpreting. The hermeneutics of suspicion, in this context, is not habitual in an inert sense, but utterly vital and transformative.

In *Ordinary Affects*, people, usually those already on the edge, find ways to survive in this precarious state, sleeping with one eye open. They dwell in a space that Berlant terms 'the impasse', which brings dimension to Stewart's 'something'. Berlant's definition of the term links this space to a necessary, everyday vigilance:

[T]he impasse is a stretch of time in which one moves around with a sense that the world is at once intensely present and enigmatic, such that the activity of living demands both a wandering absorptive awareness and a hypervigilance that collects material that might help to clarify things, maintain one's sea legs, and coordinate the standard melodramatic crises with those processes that have not yet found their genre of event. (2011: 4)

The impasse is the period where 'something' is still taking shape, coming into vision and not yet clearly defined. It is a state that signals disruption and causes anxiety, but importantly has its own structural comfort, like the proverbial calm before the storm. For some, living with the threat of doom is preferable to living with certain doom. This state of being perpetually heedful offers trepidation but also hope. Paranoid reading, then, is an everyday reading practice, armed and ready, applying its full critical attention, prepared for the worst but also hoping for reprieve. A demystifying mindset, in this case, is vital to improvisation or the creativity that survival demands.

Indeed a return to philosopher Paul Ricœur's original formulation of the 'hermeneutics of suspicion' in *Freud and Philosophy: An Essay on Interpretation* (1970) reveals that the term itself was invoked as part of a project to complicate, if not dismantle, the opposition of negative and positive positions. After tracing the hermeneutics of suspicion and the hermeneutics of faith as a received opposition, Ricœur ultimately points to the 'profound unity of the demystifying and remystifying of discourse' (1970: 54). '[T]o destroy idols, to listen to symbols,' he asks, 'are these not one and the same enterprise?' (54). Although Ricœur's term, 'the hermeneutics of suspicion', is used throughout the wider turn against critique as the apt descriptor of one side of a polemic, namely to leverage a return to positivity, in its original context Ricœur deploys it in defiance of such oppositional ways of thinking. Hermeneutics, for Ricœur, is 'animated by this double motivation: willingness to suspect and willingness to listen' (27). It is this very either/or mentality that Ricœur aims to unravel in his original analysis of the hermeneutics of suspicion.

In his study of Pynchon's novels, *Creative Paranoia: In Gravity's Rainbow* (1978), Mark Seigel notes that, for Pynchon too, paranoia is an innovating space of potential, but one which is complex rather than simply disabling or enabling. Seigel explains that, in his representations of paranoia, 'Pynchon finally promises neither annihilation nor transcendence; he is sure only that life as we know it is changing.

With creative paranoia Pynchon balances his fears for the future with his hopes' (1978: 120). Seigel adds that, to think about social dynamism pragmatically, Pynchon is not only interested in potentials, but also probabilities: '[*Gravity's Rainbow*] is a book of possibilities which seeks to divine the future through an examination of probabilities' (7). Slightly altering the Deleuzian definition that is prominent in affect theory, Pynchon's use of the term 'potential' describes more than boundless and liberating possibility.

For potential is not only about the potential for academic work to be inspiring and interesting and creative. It is about a period of indeterminacy in which people must make decisions in the dark. Social flux is not always freeing; it can create calamity. In a space of potential, people pragmatically need to infer probabilities and make adjudications to prepare for particular potentials. Novelty is informed by and responsive to history. In this practical context, the context Stewart equivocally directs us toward, reading patterns and anticipating likelihoods is vital to living social dynamism. Interpretation is intrinsic to creation, not its lagged, inert aftermath.

As Stewart's fragments infer, this method of social participation, of being wary and using one's discretion based on probabilities and existing narratives, need not dampen the potential for surprises to emerge. Probabilities do not always eventuate and known scripts can be edited by new experiences. For instance, a fragment called 'Relief' describes an experiential sense of how the paranoid frame can melt into another kind of affective response:

> Unwanted intensities simmer up at the least provocation. And then a tiny act of human kindness, or a moment of shared sardonic humor in public, can set things right again as if any sign of human contact releases an unwanted tension . . .
>
> She and Ariana are out walking in the neighborhood. White woman, brown baby. Some teenagers pass them, scowling. Brown boys dressed tough, showing attitude. But as they pass she hears one of the boys say to the others in a sweet boy's voice 'did you see that *cute* baby?' (2007: 50)

In this scene, the probabilities we carry – the wariness of a woman alone with a child and faced with a group of tough-looking young men – are happily surrendered for other affects such as renewed hope or gratefulness or surprise. Discretion is not, in this context, simply the choice between being jaded or naive.

In 'Relief', Stewart gives us a pragmatic and dynamic definition of paranoia that is more inclusive and workable than the definition she subscribes to with reference to Sedgwick and Latour. Where their definitions see paranoia as a barrier to the contingency of everyday life, particularly the productivity of belief or attachments, Stewart opens paranoia up as *the* space in which people are already navigating how truth is lived and distorted and constantly rewritten according to dynamic social currents. Stewart represents a public that makes 'something', whether it is a support group, or a conspiracy theory, or change of scene, out of both their fear *and* their hope, affects that we learn are *both* necessary to living in a society where agency is dispersed and social perimeters are contested. Stewart's ethnography therefore lends a different texture to the debate about hermeneutic methods, a scope in which paranoid reading is more than just a perfunctory reflex.

An Everyday Hermeneutics of Suspicion

In this context, Stewart's work is better served by Berlant's wary reading of reparative solutions than Sedgwick's original formulation. Berlant honours Sedgwick's vast contribution to her field and gives what is perhaps the most eloquent reading of what Sedgwick hoped to achieve with her argument 'against the hermeneutics of suspicion' (2011: 123). However, Berlant adds that, while she admires Sedgwick's dedication, she 'also resist[s] idealising, even implicitly, any program of better thought or reading' (124). 'How would we know,' she asks, 'when the "repair" we intend is not another form of narcissism or smothering will? Just because we sense it to be so?' Berlant suggests that such a proscriptive ideology, albeit dissenting, leads back to the very projection of values it hopes to avoid. In Berlant's estimation, scholars cannot afford to stop scrutinising their own evaluations and invest in a program of altruism that assumes the critic can deliver final emancipation (124).

Scholars are more likely to be among the citizens of *Ordinary Affects*: grappling curiously and hopefully for answers and often stumbling, rather than successfully and finally realising how sociality can be made fully legible. If the ethnographer is *of* the ethnographic, then it is no wonder that resonances of paranoia reverberate across sociality in a particular epoch, sounding in forms of everyday thought from the prosaic to the philosophical. In her reading of Sedgwick, Berlant tacitly repositions Stewart within the salt-of-the-earth sociality of her own ethnography, rather than with the claims to methodological succession that preface *Ordinary Affects*.

Read together, these two texts affirm that the way structure is theorised by recent critics, as a fixed and fading notion, is not representative of how people negotiate their lives or, to use Spinoza's affect schema, how they manage structuring and being structured on a day-to-day level. In the fragments of *Ordinary Affects* paranoia is not inert. It is the labour and ingenuity, the 'creative paranoia' or concomitant fear and hope that people draw upon to carve out a space for themselves – an intelligible and tellable life – amid a bustling, contested public. A demystifying and anticipatory 'paranoid reading' is no longer merely a tired and static genre, but the means by which people already try to keep up with tweaks and tremors in the social atmosphere, or how their lives are unsettled or redirected by political decisions, economic fluctuations and public events.

Citizens stay attuned to structural shifts in real time, ready to respond or revise their life story accordingly. This revision then reifies a particular structure. If we conceive of this structural negotiation on the level of genre, we can consider how the question of representation is lived in a dynamic process. Paranoia is not simply a genre of scholarly reading in this sense. It is the real-time response to and stimulation of genre shifts, reading for the markers of recognisable forms in a live, differentiating act. In this practice of social authorship, like the poets of Harold Bloom's famous study (1973), one feels an 'anxiety of influence', or the sense that one's life is also being authored by diverse authorial agents, pushed and pulled in various ways. Berlant eloquently describes this responsive act as 'the improvisation of genre amid pervasive uncertainty' (2011: 6). In this process the form an event or its repercussion will take is contingent. This living, changeable process of differentiation calls for people to respond, to stake their claim and to be ready to revise it if things do not go their way. Structuration, then, is a creative process generating its own forms of confusion and mess, but it also provides a workable scaffold for how to live or communicate.

Improvisation, here, is not an expression of uninhibited play, but an interpretive response that grapples with the threat or the pressing need to realise a liveable reality. Rather than an asocial, ineffable indeterminacy, affect emerges here as a saturating, socially generated atmosphere that pulls people into certain shapes, sometimes in ways of which they are not immediately aware. It is akin, perhaps, to Émile Durkheim's 'collective effervescence', a surge that is created and sustained by the very social it takes hold of and transforms ([1912] 2011). Affect, in this light, is not separable from causal structures or human agency or efforts to be intelligible, for it is inherent to these things.

I have argued that the fragments of *Ordinary Affects* defy some of the critical limitations set out in Stewart's introduction. Read from this perspective, Stewart's ethnography offers us a way to rethink descriptions of critique as out of touch with everyday concerns. Rather than providing an antidote to suspicion, *Ordinary Affects* provides evidence to question the need for such an antidote. Its meditation on the vigilance intrinsic to an ontology of affect troubles the division of affect from hermeneutic forms of attention. In addition, when we look at the everyday work of vigilance and inference, we see that it is not so different from the forms of critical reading scholars have used to deconstruct and reveal the inequalities that social and linguistic structures can reproduce. Following this, I propose that rather than thinking about certain methods as 'better' for engaging with affect or more immanent to social life, we might consider how affect, as a structuring capacity, informs our interest in and evaluation of particular methods over others. Our wary attention (including a wariness about critique) could be symptomatic and generative of the very world it observes. Read as structuring, affect no longer flourishes in the essential morality of one genre while eluding the feeble grasp of another: scenes of volatile life and explanatory narrative become difficult to differentiate. Critical interpretation is no longer an external distortion or a mere representation, but life itself, coalescing and refiguring its many expressions in the present. The attention in these occurrences, the paranoid reading, anticipation and inference that occurs is a creatively critical, social method. Always already contested, it is an everyday hermeneutics of suspicion, a productive act of reading that is never entirely confident of its own lens.

5

The Life of Genre

Debates about the competing verity of fact and fiction routinely ask us to decide which genre or method produces the most authentic and useful truth. I have endeavoured to ask a different question, namely how determining the rules and exclusive value of various genres might determine the kinds of truths that can be told. I was drawn to debates about affect and method because they so richly capture the paradox of desiring a raw, untrammelled truth, while also being inherently implicated in mandating what this truth can include, as well as what form it should take. The paradoxes I have uncovered in the critique of critique, therefore, need not undermine a living notion of methodology. Rather, such tensions might challenge us to revisit the logic of inclusion, differentiation and recognition that underpins intellectual work more generally. This kind of analysis carefully parses out underlying questions about where and why we draw the lines that circumscribe what will and will not qualify for a complex field, a proper genre or an affective impulse, as well as how these lines work to shape and produce particular realities.

Current methodological turns are geared toward capturing the complex flux of social life. Focusing on the people and events these genres represent, they tend to gloss over broader issues about the contingent logic with which genres are shaped. But such an inquiry needs to look at the meta-level of genre determination because the ethical problems that affect theorists seek to remedy with 'new' methods – such as didactic authorship and the reduction of life to broad and familiar categories – are inherent to, and thus reproduced by, the very act of assuming that certain methods and not others are remedial. A method does have certain affects and effects, but these are not straightforwardly static or innate. Rather, their structure and logic is affected by social desires and momentums, or disciplinary pressures and intellectual trends. The truths we can know, in this sense, are dictated by the questions we are willing to hear and ask. The intents and investments that produce tensions within social truths are evident in the very methods social scientists develop to understand or ease them. We might insist we want to recognise 'complexity', the kinds of details and relations that make categorisation difficult, but are we also selective about what we are willing to complicate? If we begin with the premise that affect and ideology are mutually exclusive, for instance, are we really asking how and why people are impelled to act?

My contention is that we need the capacity to be both critical and respectful of genre if we are to see how its dynamic, social structures are used, both knowingly and unknowingly, to verify stories or to challenge them. Paul Ricœur argued for this position in his original, and often misinterpreted, discussion of the hermeneutics of suspicion. He did not ask whether we should adopt a positive or negative form of analysis, but rather insisted upon the co-constitutive nature of faith and doubt. Ricœur ultimately points to the 'profound unity of the demystifying and remystifying of discourse' (1970: 54). Hermeneutics, he argues, is 'animated by this double motivation: willingness to suspect and willingness to listen' (27). In this closeness, negativity is seen to be inherent to creativity. In Ricœur's terms, arguments that appear oppositional are often invested in the very same pursuit that they eschew.

In the spirit of Ricœur, we must ask: how can we address the divisions that structure social life without reducing their complexity, that is respecting the gravitas of narrative propriety while also recognising the porosity, and questioning the implications, of their boundaries? How can we examine the influence of particular identities without uncritically accepting or dismissing them? To ask such a question it seems we must identify and query the impulse and pressure to reduce the terms of our ethical engagement to a neat split – be it out of convention, reverence or fear. We cannot simply be free from structure, but we can strive to become more conscious and critical of how it works, the role we play in its formation and the kinds of identities this produces and restricts. Thus, rather than claim that the means or traditions by which we differentiate fact from fiction can simply be left behind, such a consideration would also address how and why binary logic, albeit with shifting lines, is valued and reaffirmed. This chapter draws out the wider stakes of my argument for intellectual work, and offers methodological reflections on how a notion of critical affect might reorient the parameters of our arguments or unsettle our points of departure.

The Social Ethics of Genre Determination

In my effort to rethink what it is that actually identifies the limits and contours of a representational form, Bernhard Schlink's insistence that it is crucially important not to 'make this world simpler than it is' (BBC 2011) serves as an intellectual compass. As an ethics, his project challenges us to become aware of the divisions and exclusions we are complicit in, to recognise not only life's complexity, its detours and deferrals, but our inextricable involvement in the very flesh and dictation of social rules. Truth, in this consideration, is not simply given. It is alive to an ongoing and inevitably vexed process of social reckoning and recognition. As discussed in Chapter 1, Schlink encourages us to work with the tensions and unease that we may discover even if it seems more difficult or threatening to face the proximity of our implication in the very things we define ourselves against.

At the crux of Schlink's work is a provocation to scrutinise how much of the truth is verified because it affirms what we want or need in order to feel stable and coherent or to manage social life. Are there certain questions we will not ask because they risk our integrity, our work or social our cohesion at large? Opening his inquiry in a high-stakes political context, namely the German nation's conventions for remembering the Holocaust, Schlink tries to rethink the division of good and evil through the lead character in his novel *The Reader* (1997), Hanna Schmitz. As readers learn, Hanna, an Auschwitz prison guard, committed her crimes not because she was deeply and vengefully anti-Semitic, but because she was wrapped up in concealing the shame of her illiteracy and performed her professional role with thoughtless obedience. As previously explained,

Schlink's suggestion in this has met with scorn, specifically with the charge that he 'humanised' Hanna. However, Schlink sees a more troubling risk in the act of censoring all investigation into the very notion of how a category such as evil is defined. Schlink's framework challenges readers to think beyond the orderliness of binary segregations, to take in how things might be more anomalous, inconsistent or compathetic. What seems disparate may indeed be relational. The extreme polarisation of good and evil, as with the division between creation and critique, is facile and ultimately misleading.

As Schlink explains, when we maintain that people who committed crimes were 'just monsters', inhuman and immoral, we hold them too 'far away from us' and from tensions that are vital to the truth (BBC 2011). Hanna was maternal and mean, curious and ignorant, unpretentious and utterly self-absorbed. As Schlink comments, 'this is the tension we can find in people' (2011). Avery F. Gordon describes this inherent paradox as 'complex personhood', arguing that 'even those who live in the most dire circumstances possess a complex and oftentimes contradictory humanity and subjectivity that is never adequately glimpsed by viewing them as victims or, on the other hand, as superhuman agents' (2008: 4). The contradictions and tensions that Schlink and Gordon highlight, the often inconvenient details of a life, are essential to the story, though they often confound the categories we use to understand and identify people.

What is ultimately risked in polemical thinking then, for Schlink, is a true insight into the lived texture of how processes of action and accountability work across boundary lines or, in the case of *The Reader*, how Fascism specifically operated logistically and logically as a social structure. This is not to say that individual agents are blameless, or to endorse a relativist argument, but to think very carefully about how people negotiate individual and social responsibility. The question here is not whether a person is inherently good or evil, but how certain acts of exclusion became normal, or even instrumental, in people's everyday lives. What particularities or banal choices and oversights of daily life sustained the system, just as the system, with its coercive social duress, organised the particular? How did the daily actions of many Germans assume a truth or come to seem real or justified? This is a harder, more unsettling question, but arguably the most important one. To genuinely ask it requires a framework that is not wedded to, or uncritical of, explanatory structures, but rather one that recognises the role of these structures in producing particular discursive and affective conventions. In this sense, Schlink's work is a radical argument against fascistic logic, as it refuses to exclude or excise on the basis of received schemas that mark one thing from another and fix meanings. In sum, his ethical intervention provides a useful precedent for highlighting the stakes implicit in affirming or challenging the social rules and representational methods within which events or ideas can be legitimately discussed.

Following Schlink, I have analysed how genres and the rules of their propriety come to be determined on a methodological level, and tracked the ethical and authorial affects such selections produce and are produced by. Refusing to accept an essential separation between critical and affective responses, I have attempted to reveal the proximity of things that are outwardly opposed. My effort has been to both recognise and reconsider the divisions that structure polemical debates about facts and values. But beyond one debate in cultural theory, the implications of this refusal foreground the way that all stakeholders involved in a genre's determination vitally shape – with varying levels of agency – the structures and social truths that inform and govern their positions and/or selves. The study – taken away from its immediate focus – is about how we practise theory and wage arguments, or how we both presume and enact premises that can foreclose our inquiry before it begins.

What Is at Stake in the Division of Genre?

Critically aerating an either/or response to methodological debates produces new, or at least different, questions. If method is read as part of empirical messiness rather than its potential solution, the aim of innovation is no longer to hurtle toward the 'new'. Rather we might sit with the methods we presume to know so well and find new dynamism within them, or glimpse new facets illuminated by rearrangements in the social scene that animates our inquiry. The aim of *Critical Affect* then is not to resolve the rift between critical methods and affect theory, but to show how a seemingly oppositional logic both holds and unravels within these polemic proposals, producing rich relationships and crossovers. Barbara Johnson, the

American deconstructionist, speaks very eloquently on this theoretical challenge in *The Critical Difference* (1980):

> If, however, binary oppositions in this book thus play the critical
> fall guy, it is not because one must try at all costs to go beyond
> them. The very impulse to 'go beyond' is an impulse structured
> by a binary opposition between oneself and what one attempts to
> leave behind. Far from eliminating binary oppositions from the
> critical vocabulary, one can only show that binary difference does
> not function as one thinks it does and that certain subversions are
> logically prior to it and necessary to its very construction. (xi)

Of course, categories of fact and fiction exist; for Johnson, this is not
the question. The focus of inquiry is how and why these genres exist,
despite the fact they are never quite as coherent and sovereign as we
might expect. The forms of fact and fiction are politically and structurally productive, but they are not essential and fixed genres. If we
look closely their boundaries merge, shift and reify in peculiar ways.

This is why the politics of truth-telling for Schlink, or what 'lies
behind the idea that some events may not be fictionalised or may
only be fictionalised while remaining true to the facts [...] is not
about the genre [and] not about documentation versus fiction', but
'about authenticity in a fuller sense' (2009: 119). It is not, in other
words, about categorisation as a positivist project, but about the social
stakes that are invested and played out in the process of differentiating and policing particular forms. Although often underemphasised,
questions about how we mandate what does and does not properly
belong to a particular category, along with the act of selecting which
categories have value, are at the crux of debates about representational
ethics. The politics of form do not begin with the genre of the story,
with the decision of using either one genre or another, for questions
already apply to the terms by which the values and identities of such
genres have already been socially circumscribed. It is this underlying
social conflict that I have attempted to leverage: to understand what
this 'authenticity in a fuller sense' is and how it works.

Heeding Schlink's caution not to hold the identities we see to
be different from our own argument 'too far away', I have used the
method of close reading to work with the tensions within the turn

to affect. While I perceive several of the 'critique of critique's' over-sights and exclusions to be ethically problematic, I have nonetheless worked to remain close to them, 'to make myself at home in their logic', and to show that they contain their own disputes and push towards their own reparations (Kirby 2011: 86). Rather than offer-ing a separate correction, my aim has been to extend these argu-ments by drawing out the ways they already seem to extend and overturn themselves. These arguments contain what they insist they are not. They repeat what they claim to correct. It is not, therefore, that these arguments have no grasp of sociological complexity, but rather that they risk not recognising just how complex they actu-ally are. I have argued that absolute exclusion and opposition are reductive methods, sometimes unethical and often ineffective. Such an approach insists that our academic precedents and peers are not models to be cited and discarded, but ongoing sites of sociological and literary significance.

Just as Wolf Lepenies notes that Auguste Comte's efforts to make positivism a science began to resemble precisely that which Comte initially hoped to avoid, a theology, so too the 'critique of critique' often turns in what, by its own count, appears to be the wrong direction (1988: 29). The movement puts its faith in the structure of genre, assuming that the identity and capacities of fiction, for instance, are given – something upon which we all agree. However, at the same time, such methodological directives stretch these genres in such a way that they will accommodate, or exclude, whatever serves the argument about affect's autonomy and critique's redundancy, or the desired outcome for a change in social science methods. In practice, the 'affective turn' effectively proves that structure is both workably stable and malleable. Similarly, the life of evidence and verification is more provocative and unsettled than such arguments readily admit, and authorial intention, initially cast as an obstinate form of control, turns out to be strangely fickle and reflexive. In such twists and recuperations, polemical argu-ments show the risks of holding our enemies, as Schlink says, 'too far away from us', but also the impossibility of this gesture and our inevitable implication in what we prohibit.

When read closely, attempts to finally disavow or depart from a particular position, problem or method clearly falter in the arguments examined in the previous chapters. Boundaries between critique and creativity, surface and depth, affect and structure, ethics and judgement, feelings and facts, and the scholar and the social, are set up, but they nonetheless remain porous. As I have argued across the preceding chapters, with the recuperation of paranoid themes, guarded positions and a desire to advance even further into the unknown, the affective turn participates in a broader zeitgeist of detection, mystery and suspicion. Arguments for an autonomous affect, and for methods to exclusively engage it, are therefore implicated in the very crisis of representation and sceptical atmosphere they outwardly declare to be bygone.

In Stewart's ethnography *Ordinary Affects* the force and symmetry of this contradiction is almost uncanny. Just as literary theorist Sean Burke explains that 'the Death of the Author fascinates [him] as a gloriously baroque meditation on authorship' (1995: x), Stewart's argument against 'paranoid reading' reads as a 'gloriously baroque meditation' on the social vitality of suspicion. The people Stewart writes about recognise and/or struggle to recognise that they are simultaneously responsible for and vulnerable to the volatile exigencies that shape their own lives. In this text, the social, as a critical and creative body, shuffles and refigures, pushing and pulling in various directions. The arguments I have closely examined in the last three chapters are rich with a paradox and tension that opens them up to further analysis. Such analysis is often against the grain of the turn's structural divisions and intellectual direction, but it is certainly not averse to its overarching effort to create an unguarded field of inquiry. In one sense, what scholars such as Sedgwick and Latour are outwardly arguing for is the ability to ask social questions unrestricted by received schemas that make thinking less queer or accommodating than it often needs to be.

The scope for affect as a force and concept, as well as the ways we might theorise or address it, are therefore extended rather than foreclosed by my critique. If we open affect's identity up to include negativity as well as positivity or the incisive as well as the intuitive – indeed if we enlist the field of affect theory to rethink how these very received structures actually work, that is how they affect and are affected – we can extend the scope and freedom of the intended project. Affect theory, if unwedded to various exclusions, would no longer be unnecessarily divided into incompatible factions, but rather open to forging allegiances with old and new questions across disciplines and fields. In this genuinely inclusive frame, affect could be nebulous and indeterminate, but it could also be historical or linguistic or profoundly didactic, coercing the civic into certain shapes. Social scientists could find aspects to both celebrate and critique in an affect that might be dually conducive and circumspect.

Toward a Critical Affect

If we are to truly open the intellectual avenues to which the affective turn gestures, we need to take a more radical approach to inclusion, but one that looks back as well as forward. To be open to potential in a way that can, for instance, reposition Latour's uneducated conspiracist neighbour as the knowing critic and Latour as the naive believer, surely we must not begin with a host of elisions and fixed reference points that lock the common person into a position of brute wisdom and cast the intellectual as a disconnected iconoclast. Latour's own social experience, where words and social positions become strangely twisted and recast, calls for something far less polemical and rigid than this. Accordingly, I have tried to leverage some of the questions that are overlooked or excluded from such directives in order to consider how they might be re-enlisted to extend its scope. Might the barest of statistical data have the same affective influence as a poem, for instance, or might intention be something more complicated than a cognitive process that arrives, too late, at a precise and calculated moment? Instead of choosing to include either one genre or another, or the rational mind or the sensual body (as if these entities were truly separate), can we rethink the terms by which such divisions are structured? Might there be a way to reframe the notion of genre or the locus of intention so that we do not have to circumscribe our inquiry in such a way – can we include and confront the seemingly inescapable, or socially mandated, desire to make cuts, or delimit our focus, in particular ways?

When we look closely at the arguments of Latour and Sedgwick the problems of scholarship are ascribed to certain enemies, such as social science, ideology critique, social trauma from the witch hunts of the Cold War or the AIDS epidemic, the 'right wing' and, alternately, the dumbing down or obscurity of critical theory. But at the same time the recurrent motif of paranoia draws our attention to questions of reflexivity and defence, and the difficulty of locating and delineating from where threats originate or gain their strength. Aerating some of the logic with which these theorists attribute blame, it is clear that certain correlations and conflations are made. Social science, for example, is conflated with critical social theory and structural critique. This aggregate of fields is then conflated with the economic rationalist ethos of university accountants, a move which consequently seems to hold social science, and the methods it informs, accountable for budget and value cuts in the humanities. This logic is not particularly fair, nor is it helpful in isolating and really unravelling what processes are actually responsible for, or contribute to, the current realities of the academy, including potential cynicism and fatigue among thinkers.

As I have highlighted, the polarisation of the critical and the affective often inadvertently contributes to the alienation of one scholar from another and devalues the efforts of approaches which, while outwardly different, may be working toward opening similar questions or flagging shared ethical or theoretical complacencies. If we choose creative genres over critique, accepting that critique is never intuitive or inventive, then we unnecessarily limit the tools open to intellectual work, as well as the right to query and revise how the boundaries between these measures are drawn or exploited. What is truly at stake then, in rethinking notions of genre production, authorship, propriety and intention, is a way to address our own and others' complicities in narrowing the terms of our objectives to the point where we potentially thwart our ability to access revelatory alliances and illuminations. Again we meet with Schlink's caution that if we hold things away from ourselves we risk not recognising how they work or connect, how an ethics can be complicated, or how we could intervene.

It is with such challenges in mind that the question of social responsibility, at the heart of this book, merges with the question of method. For it is clear that the rules of genre are rules of life: when we examine them, we are not simply applying external frames; we are creating the very conventions, both the possibilities and limitations, by which we might think about, speak about and live life. We are deeply involved in the truths we produce. Indeed, we are produced by them. The stories we tell lend integrity to our sense of self and thus there is always a conflict of interest in storytelling, always a 'crisis of representation'. And yet, in perhaps the most fascinating tension of all, no matter how far away we position the truth, or how impossible we claim it is to access, we are still devoting our lives to the pursuit of it, in various ways. Even radically post-human arguments still pursue the most authentic way to account for life and how it is constituted. As Gordon explains, '[w]arnings about relativism to the contrary, truth is still what most of us strive for. Partial and insecure surely, and something slightly different from "the facts," but truth nonetheless: the capacity to say "This is so"' (Gordon 2008: 2). The question of method then is not just about how we can capture the texture of social complexity, but how we can account for our participation in the intricate authorship of social life, especially in determining which field or questions can be complicated. The ethics of truth-telling, in this light, requires us to consider how we live truth, not just how best to represent it. How can we make sense of social knots when our investigations further tangle and unravel their threads? How can we attend to and become responsible for our involvement in the complex social systems, the very regimes of recognition and differentiation, that we seek to understand and transform?

To break from either/or thinking without presuming this is a final or radical break is one challenge, and to recognise one's own involvement is another. The question for social science then is not just how to recognise the complex nature of affective life, as if it were simply there waiting to be revealed, but how our own inquiry affects and is affected by conventions of recognition. How can one take a critical position, or claim an identity, when we, and the terms by which we define ourselves, are always in flux? Vital to this inquiry is the question of why and how we invest in moral and social divisions and how we reaffirm them, knowingly or not. Such a position will also require acknowledging the inevitable blind spots of our own, nonetheless crucial, differentiations. For Schlink, it is clear that the facts of the past are inseparable from the values inherent in how we recount them today, just as identity is bound to its representation. Thus, in remembering history, we are ultimately faced with the challenge of understanding the ongoing social authorship in which we remain present: to read a story that, in our very act of comprehending and responding, we are also continuing, in various ways, to refigure and reaffirm.

Drawing out this implication in *The Things They Saved: Pieces of a Jewish Past* (2011), Nancy K. Miller recounts the experience of tracing her family tree and finding things that radically altered the stories she knew about her family, and thus how she is positioned by these same stories. This investment in how the story will unfold – Miller's very involvement in its implications – leads her to discover that a form of self-reflexivity, though always problematised, is vital to her process of re-membering history. It is not just the story that holds tensions, but Miller's own method of reading it. 'Despite my intense desire to know the truth, however partial or incomplete,' Miller explains, 'I am forced to recognise that the process of finding the story continues to change the story. As I advance into the territory of recovery, I can't trust even myself. That may be the hardest lesson of all' (26). Tracing her genealogy, Miller practises a hermeneutics of suspicion: asking the question of truth and of method. To be present to the contingency of this method, to be wary not only of the knowledge we interpret but also of our act of interpretation, is, as Miller argues, perhaps 'the hardest lesson of all'. Such a lesson calls for us to acknowledge our own relation to truth, our complicity in both its openness and vulnerability, and its incredible power to both exclude and produce, often at the same time. Such a lesson makes us wary of how the truths we tell are authored and why they are desired. Rather than resolving which genre produces the most truthful account, we are left with questions about where a story's authorship originates and by whom or what it is impelled. What do we require of truths? And can we always recognise our role in negotiating their verification? The idea that we would set aside a focus on epistemology to engage with ontology risks missing how some of the most pressing ontological questions are about how we experience and navigate methods of truth-telling.

Emotional Truth and the Method of Politics

In Chapter 1 I traced a brief genealogy of the two cultures through a series of 'crises of representation'. Following this lineage into the present, we now face another proclaimed crisis around the production of truths. In what is being called the 'post-truth age', clickbait, fake news and 'alternative facts' are shared in the civic sphere, from political podiums and within social media filter bubbles – 'a hyper-emotional environment of visceral reactions and paranoid instincts' (Hannan 2018: 222). This current debate again divides factual truths and emotional truths as two distinct genres, yet it also presents us with a messier reality where people patch together accounts across party lines. Crucially, in this context, conversations about how truths are decided are not solely the domain of ivory tower speculation. The affective aspects of truth and method feature in discussions about media literacy, political beliefs and social inclusion. With the relationship between emotion and truth at the centre of both academic and social concern, we have an opportunity to carefully consider the stakes of thinking with and across polemical structures. This, again, is not a matter of choosing sides, but rather attending to how sides are determined via acts of telling and hearing truths. In this approach we pitch our inquiry at the level of genre determination rather than at the level of accepted forms. In the context of 'post-truth', the task is a difficult one: how can we break from either/or thinking when the political and structural terms of debate become ever more polemic? How can we work with methods – including our own – in a way that recognises their own unique logic and affects, yet does not curtail the potential for critical engagement? How can we define emotion and evidence in ways that do not immediately seek to oppose them or see methods as live, processual events that are not fixed and already known?

The academic argument that affect is more dynamic and true to lived experience, and that critique is knowing and dismissive, sits comfortably with the current polemic around expertise in public culture. However, the arena of post-truth, with its intricate entanglement of facts and values, hermeneutics and intuition, ideology and affect, and diverse ways of feeling suspicious, calls for a less polemic division of critical and affective approaches as well as close attention to how genres are determined. As speech acts that appeal to emotion increasingly animate political life, attending to affect is vital for social science now, but critical questions about why genres come to be either prized or suspected remain crucial to its study.

In current debates about truth-telling the question of genre sits at the forefront. The 'post-truth era' is described as a time when different modes of verification – including emotional truth – vie for legitimacy.

The term denotes a social environment where a distrust of established institutions elevates emotional appeals as seemingly more authentic and dialogic modes of communication. As its 2016 'word of the year', the *Oxford English Dictionary* defines 'post-truth' as 'relating to or denoting circumstances in which objective facts are less influential in shaping public opinion than appeals to emotion and personal belief' (OED 2016). This shift has implications for what genres of truth-telling are seen to be effective or what style of reporting will make people pay attention. A brief by Natalia Banulescu-Bogdan from the US Migration Policy Institute entitled 'When Facts Don't Matter' (2018), for example, advises policy-makers that presenting facts and figures to dispel misinformation often backfires, especially if the facts go against people's personal beliefs. The brief argues that this distrust stems from a wider loss of faith in expertise. It explains that 'the wave of support for politicians touting populist positions' and 'a growing disdain for academic institutions and a skepticism of the experts they produce' has meant that 'messages conveyed by politicians through emotional appeals may be seen as more authentic than those backed up by research' (Banulescu-Bogdan 2018: 1). Here modes of critique and suspicion are seen to be elite, authoritarian and dismissive of felt truths. But while emotion may be read as the raw truth – an unmediated gut reaction – all genres of truth-telling sculpt and elicit faith in different ways. A renewed emphasis on 'emotional truth' signals that scholars need to take seriously everyday modes of sense-making and intuition, but also notice how affect can operate within strategic and lucrative political processes. It calls for us to examine the productive force of emotion, but also how emotions can be elicited to generate power, and not necessarily power for the people that feel them.

Sociologist Arlie Hochschild writes about *how* the emotional truths spoken by politicians resonate with constituents. In this *how* we see affect and narratives become entangled and verify daily choices. It also becomes clear why this process calls for scrutiny – when feeling is hastily accepted as a more authentic mode of knowing we can miss the ways that emotion and affect work structurally to include and exclude, or how an affective current moves in ways that can leave people unmoored. As research for *Strangers in Their Own Land: Anger and Mourning on the American Right* (2016), Hochschild spent time at the homes and churches of Tea Party Republicans in the lead-up to the 2016 US presidential election. She asked these voters how they came to hold their political beliefs and how they reconciled, for example, concern about the pollution of local rivers with support for a political party that lobbies to deregulate environmental protections. What Hochschild describes is the emotional construction of a political polemic. While she focuses on the right in this study, she acknowledges the need for a similarly close analysis of the deep stories held by the Berkeley liberals that make up her own milieu. In speaking to people who hold beliefs counter to her own, Hochschild's aim is, in the spirit of Schlink, 'not to hold people too far away from us', and to closely examine how affect structures people's sense of what is true.

In the deep south Hochschild found that the echo chamber effect of tabloid media contributed to people's viewpoints, with Fox News buzzing in the background on television sets. But she also noticed that the incendiary slant on these channels resonated with what she calls listeners' 'deep stories' (135). The deep story is shared yet very personal, and taps into family and local history (51). It makes sense of why people are less wealthy and secure than their ancestors were, when it should be the other way around. It rallies people who are in the same boat, who are also losing out in an ostensibly zero-sum game, where elite liberals let migrants come in and squeeze welfare and take jobs from long-standing, hard-working Americans (137). It gives people false reasons for real deprivation. Nonetheless, the deep story gets repeated over and over, at home and at work and at church. It is profoundly affective and constructs what Hochschild calls an 'empathy wall' (5–8), which keeps in people who feel the same and keeps out people who feel differently. While several of the voters Hochschild speaks to have concerns that run counter to the party line, these critiques are ultimately overcome by the emotional appeal of the deep story and the greater stakes it represents – as a source of identity, belonging and an explanation for life's hardships.

The creation of shared affects, in this context, has profoundly structural sources and implications. For example, the appeal to people's emotions and cherished convictions has played a role in the political campaigns of US President Donald Trump, but also of other populist figures such as England's Nigel Farage and France's Marine Le Pen. These politicians have all mobilised support and attempted to discredit their opponents via the design and spread of often deliberately divisive 'fake news'. To give just two examples of this mendacity, in the lead up to the 2017 French election, Le Pen's social media team spread fake news that rival candidate Emmanuel Macron kept a secret offshore bank account in the luxurious Bahamas; and while campaigning for Brexit, Farage brazenly touted bogus figures including that the European Union had created 75 per cent of Britain's laws and that the EU costs British taxpayers £350 million per week (Hannan 2018; Gerbaudo 2018). What shared narratives, or 'deep stories', we might ask, do these trumped-up claims resonate with? Many scholars have written with concern about the social costs of 'fake news' and misinformed citizens. Vian Bakir and Andrew McStay (2018), for example, argue that 'deliberately affective' fake news misinforms citizens who are 'likely to stay wrongly informed in [social media] echo chambers' where, it is assumed, others hold the same views and desire the same political outcomes, and are therefore unlikely to challenge or correct them (6). In these arguments it is assumed that shared emotions verify and support ongoing faith in fake news.

But if we are to take the affective purchase of verifying methods seriously, it is important, as Bruno Latour cautions, not to assume that people are simply being tricked en masse (2005). Hochschild also notes that 'as an explanation for why any of us believe in what we do, duping – and the presumption of gullibility – is too simple an idea' (2017: 14). While emerging studies of 'fake news' literacy demonstrate that it *is* sometimes the case that people cannot readily distinguish between real and fabricated news sources (Romano 2017; Bakir and McStay 2018; Tandoc et al. 2018; Boyd-Barrett 2019), Susan Krasmann (2018) raises a slightly more complex picture in her work on post-truth regimes. Her concern is not that people are being fooled, but that people often know such claims to be false yet endorse them for what they *do* – namely rattle the upstanding properness of news media and political speech-making. Such a speech acts draws affective energy from how it plays with the assumed propriety of truth-telling genres.

In this frame, Trump appeals not because his lies are taken as facts (though this may also be part of it), but because his lies are taken as an irreverent exercise of anti-authoritarian power. As Krasmann writes, from the outset of Trump's presidency, in innumerable tweets and speeches:

> [H]e was obviously making false or misleading claims. [. . .] [A]s a constant source of public incredulity, these claims were perceived as irritating if not disconcerting, as they gave the public an idea of the president's unreliability; depending on the point of view, they did not fail, however, to also diffuse an ambience of exhilaration, if not admiration, as they conspicuously displayed a new political game of un-truthfulness. (6)

This 'game of untruthfulness' is doubled when Trump readily accuses other politicians and commentators of spreading fake news when they criticise him, often in ways that are quite clearly substantiated. By lying and accusing others of lying, Trump, as Krasmann points out, is not just manipulating the truth, but also the *methods* of truth-telling and verification that underpin democratic political systems and news media.[1] Playing this 'game of un-truthfulness', he casts the earnest pursuit of transparency and fact-checking as a tool the political elite and mainstream media use to discredit the stated concerns of ordinary people. Linguist Jayson Harsin writes that in an arena where 'socio-institutional truth and trust deficits have become so great' (2018: 512), the task of translation requires attention to new 'dispositions toward truth-telling' (512). Trump's speech is difficult to translate because its sense lies in what it *does* rather than what it says. His use of emotional truth makes it hard to capture the wider context that gives his words impact, or the deep stories that he taps into. Similarly, if we, as scholars, simply divide critical from emotional appeals we overlook the mechanics of how shared affect fuels Trump's critique of the establishment and, at the very same time, shields this (established) critic from his own accusations.

---

[1] We need to be wary perhaps of claiming that such 'games of un-truthfulness' are a wholly 'new' state of affairs, as Hannah Arendt notes in 'Lying in Politics' (1972) '[t]he deliberate falsehood and the outright lie, used as legitimate means to achieve political ends have been with us since the beginning of recorded history' (4). But this resurgence of interest in emotional truth offers up another opportunity to think with and through the binaries that set critique and affect apart.

Rereading Difference

Lending itself less easily to the idea of 'good' affect and 'bad' affect, the shape-shifting nimbleness of emotional truths requires us not to assume that critique is exhausted and affect is remedial. In the proposals I have read closely in *Critical Affect* we are told to be wary of critique and its guiding suspicions, to resist the desire to be knowing, to demystify or to put too much faith in the revelatory power of poststructural models of reading. We are told that what is more relevant, for this moment, are modes of creative and affective attunement that give real weight to everyday concerns and feelings. We are advised not to analyse and judge events as they unfold, looking to expose underlying agency and cause, but rather to attend to aesthetic particulars, affordances or what happens on the surface. As I have illustrated, the structure of this argument posits two very different methodological orientations toward social life. But in a social scene where critiques are laden with affect, where affects are the motor of critiques and where playing with modes of truth and verification is commonplace, this division collapses. In our increasingly divisive political spheres, differences are stubborn and real. They have profound effects in the world – igniting racism and hardening borders. But differences are also changeable and re-determined in the very acts of making and/or denying differentiations.

Attending to this seeming paradox is how Barbara Johnson argues we can arrive at a mode of reading that is both critical and generous. For her, deconstruction is not about dismissing difference but about attending closely to how difference works, often in ways that reveal how it is maintained and what is at stake in this maintenance. Johnson writes that: 'The "deconstruction" of a binary opposition is thus not an annihilation of all values and differences; it is an attempt to follow the subtle, powerful effects of differences already at work within the illusion of a binary opposition' (1980: xi). What seems to be firmly either/or, upon closer examination often turns out to be fraught with internal struggle, held together only through tenuous reliance on a reductive view of its constructed opponent. This can be true of political factions and of academic turns.

My aim in *Critical Affect* is not to prescribe yet another new method. Rather I have tried to offer a critical reading that reorients current thinking but allows us to stay where we are, albeit in a way that is more tentative and less censorious about where we sit in relation to past works. In this regard, close reading might be as a good a mode as any to begin rethinking how we define critique or affect. If we work critically with close reading we may find it offers more than the hasty assessments that Felski or Best and Marcus, for example, make, when they cast it off as a 'nostalgic' (Best and Marcus 2009: 1–2) or 'shop-worn' fashion (Felski 2008: 1). It is true that the Cold War has passed, but how might a productive suspicion or a desire to demystify, even if we take critique to be limited to just these affects, be reanimated now in response to post-truth and the distrust of expertise? How might the *use* of this dynamic method transform it? Rather than assuming that such modes of scholarship, supposedly grasping onto a deluded faith in erudite analysis, must be replaced by practice-based actions that mirror the concerns of citizens, can we think more critically about how and why methods come to hold, or lose, value? What drives our preference for the new, or our desire to be at the forefront, or to perform a generational succession?

Social scientists tend to describe the contemporary world as increasingly fluid, fast-paced, accelerated. But as the persistence of the two cultures demonstrates, sometimes structures endure, though we may not immediately recognise their shifting guises. This con-stancy is also dynamic, offering difference in repetition. It requires looking back and looking twice. Johnson quotes Roland Barthes's take on the value of rereading over the tendency to catapult toward the new. 'Rereading', Barthes says, is 'an operation contrary to the commercial and ideological habits of our society, which would have us "throw away" the story once it has been consumed ("devoured"), so that we can then move onto another story, buy another book' (Barthes, in Johnson 1980: 3). But he argues that 'rereading [. . .] alone saves the text from repetition (those who fail to reread are obliged to read the same story everywhere)' (in 1980: 3). Just as Schlink notes that when we hold something far away from us we deny its complexity, Johnson, following Barthes, argues that 'When we read a text once [. . .] we can see in it only what we have already learned to see before' (1980: 3). We assume we already know the genre and therefore know the story. To reread, to *stay with* a story, is to notice how it works with and against genre, or to see the ways it is unknown. This rereading is open to novelty and surprise, but without the need to dismiss or demote or to trade in the old for the new.

I have aimed to show how staying with a turn, working critically with it rather than turning once again, can reorient the parameters of how we engage with past work. Here affect emerges as a concept that can inform enduring questions about truth and evidence and what it means to *know* something. To think about the relationship between affect and truth-telling can teach us about the structural aspects of affect, the way it operates narratively, tapping into deep stories and reifying dormant divides. When not opposed to the linguistic turn, affect can inform questions of language and representational ethics, opening unseen kinships and shared questions across schools of thought. A critical approach to affect also reveals and tests the determinants of how the concept is drawn, how it is given leverage and value. We are alerted to the level of method, and the means by which we set out the capacities of what a method can do. In this light, we see how all genres, all modes of seeking and telling 'the story', are continually refigured by shifts in social sentiment and trust. To assume that each genre has a static and limited affect, for example that critique is paranoid and novels are enchanting, misses how our modes of looking and representing react and respond to the past, the present and the futures that we anticipate. Their affective texture and force are determined in a dynamic, processual way that changes as the rules for how we recognise, order and verify the empirical world are revised by politicians, citizens and a wider ecology in ways that demand both credible and critical attention.

Bibliography

Aagaard, Jesper (2018), 'Striving for experiential resonance: critique, postcritique, and phenomenology', *Qualitative Studies*, 5: 1, 29–38.

Ablow, Rachael (ed.) (2010), *The Feeling of Reading: Affective Experience and Victorian Literature*. Ann Arbor: University of Michigan Press.

Adorno, Theodor ([1951] 2005), *Minima Moralia: Reflections on a Damaged Life*. London and New York: Verso.

Ahmed, Sara (2014), *The Cultural Politics of Emotion*, 2nd edn. Edinburgh: Edinburgh University Press.

Althusser, Louis and Balibar, Etienne ([1970] 1979), *Reading Capital*. London: Verso.

Anderson, Ben (2014), *Encountering Affect: Capacities, Apparatuses, Conditions*. London: Routledge.

Apter, Emily (2006), 'On oneworldedness: or paranoia as a world system', *American Literary History*, 18: 2, 365–89.

Arendt, Hannah (1972), 'Lying in Politics', in *Crises of the Republic*. New York: Harcourt, pp. 1–48.

Aristotle and Else, Gerald F. (1967), *Aristotle: Poetics*. Ann Arbor: University of Michigan Press.

Ashman, Keith M. and Barringer, Philip S. (eds) (2000), *After the Science Wars*. London: Routledge.

Auper, Stef (2012), '"Trust No One": modernisation, paranoia and conspiracy culture', *European Journal of Communication*, 27: 1, 22–34.

Aurelius, Marcus (1998), *The Meditations of Marcus Aurelius Antoninus*, trans. John Jackson. Oxford: Clarendon Press.

Bakhtin, Mikhail. M. (1986), *Speech Genres and Other Late Essays*, trans. Vern W. McGee. Austin: University of Texas Press.

Bakir, Vian and McStay, Andrew (2018), 'Fake news and the economy of emotions: problems, causes, solutions', *Digital Journalism*, 6: 2, 154–75.

Banulescu-Bogdan, Natalia (2018), *When Facts Don't Matter: How to Communicate More Effectively about Immigration's Costs and Benefits*. Washington, DC: Migration Policy Institute.

Barad, Karen (2007), *Meeting the Universe Halfway: Quantum Physics and the Entanglement of Matter and Meaning*. Durham, NC and London: Duke University Press.

Barnwell, Ashley (2015), 'Enduring divisions: critique, method, and questions of value in the sociology of literature', *Cultural Sociology*, 9: 4, 550–66.

Barnwell, Ashley (2018), 'Durkheim as affect theorist', *Journal of Classical Sociology*, 18: 1, 21–35.

Barthes, Roland (1980), *Camera Lucida: Reflections of Photography*, trans. Richard Howard. New York: Hill & Wang.

Baudrillard, Jean (2003), *The Spirit of Terrorism and Other Essays*. London and New York: Verso.

BBC World Book Club (2011), Bernhard Schlink – *The Reader*, broadcast 2 January 2011, online: <http://www.bbc.co.uk/programmes/p00cp7t1> (accessed 20 May 2019).

Behar, Ruth and Gordon, Deborah A. (1995), *Women: Writing Culture*. Berkeley: University of California Press.

Benjamin, Walter (1968), 'On some motifs in Baudelaire', in *Illuminations*. New York: Schocken Books, pp. 155–200.

Benjamin, Walter (1983), *Charles Baudelaire: A Lyric Poet in the Era of High Capitalism*. London: Verso.

Bennett, Jane (2010), *Vibrant Matter: A Political Ecology of Things*. Durham, NC and London: Duke University Press.

Berlant, Lauren (2008), *The Female Complaint: The Unfinished Business of Sentimentality in American Culture*. Durham, NC and London: Duke University Press.

Berlant, Lauren (2011), *Cruel Optimism*. Durham, NC and London: Duke University Press.

Bersani, Leo (1989), 'Pynchon, paranoia, and literature', *Representations*, 25: 1, 99–118.

Best, Stephen (2017), 'La foi postcritique, on second thought', *PMLA*, 132: 2, 337–43.

Best, Stephen and Marcus, Sharon (2009) 'Surface Reading: An Introduction', *Representations*, Special Issue: 'The Way We Read Now', 108: 1, 1–21.

Best, Susan (2011), *Visualizing Feeling: Affect and the Feminine Avant-garde*. London: I. B. Tauris.

Bewes, Timothy (2010), 'Reading with the grain: a new world in literary criticism', *differences*, 21: 3, 1–33.

Bisson, L. A. (1945), 'Proust, Bergson, and George Eliot', *Modern Language Review*, 40: 2, 104–14.

Blackman, Lisa (2012), *Immaterial Bodies: Affect, Embodiment, Mediation*. Thousand Oaks: Sage.

Blackman, Lisa and Venn, Couze (2010), 'Affect', *Body & Society*, 16: 1, 7–28.

Bloom, Harold (1973), *The Anxiety of Influence: A Theory of Poetry*. Oxford: Oxford University Press.

Bloom, Harold (2003), 'Dumbing down American readers', *Boston Globe*, 24 September 2003.

Boland, Tom (2019), *The Spectacle of Critique: From Philosophy to Cacophony*. London: Routledge.

Bourdieu, Pierre (1984), *Distinction: A Social Critique of the Judgement of Taste*, trans. Richard Nice. Cambridge, MA: Harvard University Press.

Boyd-Barrett, Oliver (2019), 'Fake news and "RussiaGate" discourses: propaganda in the post-truth era', *Journalism*, 20: 1, 87–91.

Boynton, Robert S. (2005), *The New New Journalism: Conversations with America's Nonfiction Writers on Their Craft*. New York: Vintage Books.

Brennan, Teresa (2003), *The Transmission of Affect*. Ithaca: Cornell University Press.

Brennan, Timothy (2010), 'Running and dodging: the rhetoric of doubleness in contemporary theory', *New Literary History*, 41: 2, 277–99.

Burke, Sean (1995), *Authorship: From Plato to the Postmodern*. Edinburgh: Edinburgh University Press.

Butler, Judith (2002), 'What is critique? An essay on Foucault's virtue', in *The Political*, ed. David Ingram. Oxford: Blackwell, pp. 212–26.

Butler, Judith (2012), 'Precarious life, vulnerability, and the ethics of cohabitation', *Journal of Speculative Philosophy*, 26: 2, 134–51.

Chiew, Florence and Barnwell, Ashley (2019), 'Methodological intimacies and the figure of the twins, *Sociological Review*, 67: 2, 467–80.

Clifford, James and Marcus, George E. (eds) (1986), *Writing Culture: The Poetics and Politics of Ethnography*. Berkeley: University of California Press.

Clough, Patricia Ticineto (2007), *The Affective Turn: Theorizing the Social*. Durham, NC: Duke University Press.

CNN Larry King live transcript (2006), Interview with James Frey, aired 11 January, online: <http://transcripts.cnn.com/TRANSCRIPTS/0601/11/lkl.01.html> (accessed 20 May 2019).

Connolly, William E. (2002), *Neuropolitics: Thinking, Culture, Speed*. Minneapolis: University of Minnesota Press.

Cordle, Daniel (1999), *Postmodern Postures: Literature, Science and the Two Cultures Debate*. Aldershot: Ashgate.

Dahmen, Nicole S. (2010), 'Construction of the truth and destruction of *A Million Little Pieces*: framing in the editorial response to the James Frey case', *Journalism Studies*, 11: 1, 115–30.

Darwin, Charles, Ekman, Paul and Prodger, Phillip (1998), *The Expression of the Emotions in Man and Animals*, 3rd edn. London: Harper Collins.

Davis, Elynor G. (1985), 'Mill, socialism and the English romantics: an interpretation', *Economica New Series*, 52: 207, 345–58.

Davis, Lennard J. (1987), *Resisting Novels: Ideology and Fiction*. London: Routledge.

de Peuter, Greig (2011), 'Creative economy and labor precarity: a contested convergence', *Journal of Communication Inquiry*, 35: 4, 417–25.

Deleuze, Gilles and Guattari, Félix (1994), 'Immanence: a life', in *What Is Philosophy?* New York: Columbia University Press, pp. 25–33.

Deleuze, Gilles and Guattari, Félix (2000), 'Percept, affect, concept', in *The Continental Aesthetics Reader*, ed. Clive Cazeaux. London and New York: Routledge, pp. 484–507.

Derrida, Jacques (1987), *The Post Card: From Socrates to Freud and Beyond*. Chicago: University of Chicago Press.

Desan, Philippe, Ferguson, Priscilla Parkhurst and Griswold, Wendy (eds) (1989), *Literature and Social Practice*. Chicago: University of Chicago Press.

Descartes, René ([1649] 1984), 'The Passions of the Soul', in *The Philosophical Writings of Descartes*, Vol. 1, trans. John Cottingham,

Robert Stoothoff and Dugald Murdoch. Cambridge: Cambridge University Press, pp. 325–404.

Devitt, Amy J. (2004), 'A theory of genre', *Writing Genres*. Carbondale: Southern Illinois University Press, pp. 1–32.

Dickens, Charles (1854), *Hard Times*. London: Wordsworth Classic Editions.

Doctorow, E. L. (1977), 'False documents', *American Review*, 26, 215–32.

Dolphijn, Rick and van der Tuin, Iris (2012), *New Materialism: Interviews and Cartographies*. London: Open Humanities Press.

Durkheim, Émile ([1897] 1970), *Suicide: A Study in Sociology*. London: Routledge & Kegan Paul.

Durkheim, Émile ([1895] 1982), *The Rules of the Sociological Method*, trans. W. D. Halls. New York: Free Press.

Durkheim, Émile ([1912] 2011), *The Elementary Forms of Religious Life*. Oxford: Oxford University Press.

English, James F. (2010), 'Everywhere and nowhere: the sociology of literature after "the sociology of literature"', *New Literary History*, Special Issue: 'The Sociology of Literature', 41: 2, v–xxiii.

Fassin, Didier (2017), 'The endurance of critique', *Anthropological Theory*, 17: 1, 4–29.

Felski, Rita (2008), *Uses of Literature*. Malden, MA and Oxford: Blackwell.

Felski, Rita (2009), 'After suspicion', *Profession*, pp. 28–35.

Felski, Rita (2011a), 'Critique and the hermeneutics of suspicion', *M/C Journal*, 15: 1, online: <http://journal.mediaculture.org.au/index.php/mcjournal/article/view/431> (accessed 15 October 2017).

Felski, Rita (2011b), 'Suspicious minds', *Poetics Today*, 32: 2, 216–34.

Felski, Rita (2015), *The Limits of Critique*. Chicago: University of Chicago Press.

Fenster, Mark (2008), *Conspiracy Theories: Secrecy and Power in American Culture*. Minneapolis and London: University of Minnesota Press.

Ferguson, Priscilla Parkhurst, Desan, Philippe and Griswold, Wendy (1988), 'Editors' introduction: mirrors, frames, and demons: reflections on the sociology of literature', *Critical Inquiry*, 14: 3, 421–30.

Fielding, K. J. (1956), 'Mill and Gradgrind', *Nineteenth-Century Fiction*, 11: 2, 148–51.

Forster, E. M. (1954), *Aspects of the Novel*. Cambridge: Harcourt Brace Jovanovich.

Foucault, Michel ([1978] 2002), 'What is critique?', *Political: Readings in Continental Philosophy*, ed. David Ingram. London: Basil Blackwell, pp. 191–211.

Frank, Adam and Wilson, Elizabeth A. (2012), 'Like-minded', *Critical Inquiry*, 38, 870–7.

Fraser, Miriam (2009), 'Experiencing Sociology', *European Journal of Social Theory*, 12: 1, 63–81.

Freud, Sigmund ([1916] 2003), *The Uncanny*, trans. David McLintock. New York: Penguin Books.

Frey, James (2003), *A Million Little Pieces*. New York: Doubleday.

Friedman, Susan Stanford (2017), 'Both/and: critique and discovery in the humanities', *PMLA*, 132: 2, 344–51.

Frow, John (2006), *Genre: The New Critical Idiom*. London: Routledge.

Geertz, Clifford (1980), 'Blurred genres: the reconfiguration of social thought', *American Scholar*, 49: 2, 165–79.

Gerbaudo, Paolo (2018), 'Social media and populism: an elective affinity?', *Media, Culture & Society*, 40: 5, 745–53.

Gibbs, Anna (2005), 'Fictocriticism, affect, mimesis: Engendering differences', *TEXT*, 9: 1, online: <http://www.textjournal.com.au/april05/gibbs.html> (accessed 30 May 2017).

Goethe, J. W. ([1774] 2006), *The Sorrows of Young Werther*. New York and Berlin: Mondial Books.

Goffman, Erving (1959), *The Presentation of Self in Everyday Life*. New York: Doubleday.

Goffman, Erving (1961), *Asylums: Essays on the Social Situation of Mental Patients and Other Inmates*. New York: Doubleday.

Goldman, H. S. (1988), *Max Weber and Thomas Mann: Calling and the Shaping of the Self*. Los Angeles: University of California Press.

Goldman, H. S. (1992), *Politics, Death, and the Devil: Self and Power in Max Weber and Thomas Mann*. Los Angeles: University of California Press.

Gordon, Avery F. (2008), *Ghostly Matters: Haunting and the Sociological Imagination*, 2nd edn. Minneapolis and London: University of Minnesota Press.

Gorton, Kristyn (2007), 'Theorizing emotion and affect: feminist engagements', *Feminist Theory*, 8: 3, 333–48.

Gregg, Melissa and Seigworth, Gregory J. (2010), *The Affect Theory Reader*. Durham, NC: Duke University Press.

Guralnick, Peter (1995), *Last Train to Memphis: The Rise of Elvis Presley*. London: Abacus Press.

Hannan, Jason (2018), 'Trolling ourselves to death? Social media and post-truth politics', *European Journal of Communication*, 33: 2, 214–26.

Haraway, Donna (2007), *When Species Meet*. Minneapolis: University of Minnesota Press.

Hardt, M. and Negri, A. (2009), *Commonwealth*. Cambridge: Belknap.

Harman, Graham (2018), *Object-Oriented Ontology: A New Theory of Everything*. London: Penguin.

Harsin, Jayson (2015), 'Trump l'œil: is Trump's post-truth communication translatable?', *Contemporary French and Francophone Studies*, 21: 5, 512–22.

Hawthorn, Geoffrey (1976), *Enlightenment and Despair: A History of Sociology*. Cambridge and New York: Cambridge University Press.

Heilbron, Johan (1995), *The Rise of Social Theory*. Cambridge: Polity Press.

Hemmings, Claire (2006), 'Invoking affect', *Cultural Studies*, 19: 5, 548–67.

Henry, Matthew A. (1997), 'Problemized narratives: history as fiction in E. L. Doctorow's "Billy Bathgate"', *CRITIQUE: Studies in Contemporary Fiction*, 39: 1, 32–41.

Hersh, Seymour M. (2004), *Chain of Command: The Road from 9/11 to Abu Ghraib*. London and New York: HarperCollins.

Highmore, Ben (2011), *Ordinary Lives: Studies in the Everyday*. London and New York: Routledge.

Hobbes, Thomas ([1651] 1994), *Leviathan, with Selected Variants from the Latin Edition of 1668,* ed. E. Curley. Indianapolis: Hackett.

Hochschild, Arlie (2016), *Strangers in Their Own Land: Anger and Mourning on the American Right*. London: New Press.

Hockey, Jennifer Lorna and Dawson, Andrew (1997), *After Writing Culture: Epistemology and Praxis in Contemporary Anthropology*. New York: Routledge.

Holmes, Douglas R. (1999), 'Tactical thuggery: National Socialism in the East End of London', in *Paranoia Within Reason: A Casebook on Conspiracy as Explanation*, ed. George Marcus. Chicago: University of Chicago Press, pp. 319–41.

Hume, Kathryn (2000), 'Books of the dead: postmortem politics in novels by Mailer, Burroughs, Acker, and Pynchon', *Modern Philology*, 97: 3, 417–44.

Illouz, Eva (2007), *Cold Intimacies: The Making of Emotional Capitalism.* Cambridge: Polity Press.

Jameson, Fredric (1984), 'Postmodernism, or the cultural logic of late capitalism', *New Left Review*, 146, 53–92.

Jameson, Fredric (1992), *Postmodernism, or, the Cultural Logic of Late Capitalism.* Durham, NC: Duke University Press.

Johnson, Barbara (1980), *The Critical Difference: Essays in the Contemporary Rhetoric of Reading.* Baltimore and London: Johns Hopkins University Press.

Kirby, Vicki (2011), *Quantum Anthropologies: Life at Large.* Durham, NC and London: Duke University Press.

Knauft, Bruce (2006), 'Anthropology in the middle', *Anthropological Theory*, 6, 407–30.

Knight, Peter (ed.) (2002), *Conspiracy Nation: The Politics of Paranoia in Postwar America.* New York and London: New York University Press.

Krakauer, Jon (1996), *Into the Wild.* Basingstoke and Oxford: Pan Books.

Krasmann, Susanne (2018), 'Secrecy and the forces of truth: countering post-truth regimes', *Cultural Studies*, 33: 4, 690–71.

La Caze, Marguerite and Lloyd, Henry Martyn (2011), 'Editors' introduction: Philosophy and the "affective turn"', *Parrhesia*, 13, 1–13.

Latour, Bruno (2004), 'Why has critique run out of steam? From matters of fact to matters of concern', *Critical Inquiry*, 30, 225–48.

Latour, Bruno (2005), *Reassembling the Social: An Introduction to Actor-Network-Theory.* Oxford: Oxford University Press.

Latour, Bruno (2010), 'An attempt at a compositionist manifesto', online: <http://www.bruno-latour.fr/articles/article/120-COM-POMANIFESTO.pdf> (accessed 18 March 2018).

Latour, Bruno and Woolgar, Steve (1979), *Laboratory Life: The Social Construction of Scientific Facts.* Beverly Hills, CA: Sage.

Laurenson, Diana and Swingewood, Alan (1972), *The Sociology of Literature.* London: Paladin.

Law, John (2004), *After Method: Mess in Social Science Research.* New York: Routledge.

Law, John and Hassard, John (eds) (1999), *Actor Network Theory and After*. Malden, MA: Blackwell.

Leavis, F. R. ([1962] 2013), *Two Cultures? The Significance of C. P. Snow*. Cambridge: Cambridge University Press.

Lepenies, Wolf (1988), *Between Literature and Science: The Rise of Sociology*. Cambridge and New York: Cambridge University Press.

Leys, Ruth (2011), 'The turn to affect: a critique', *Critical Inquiry*, 37: 3, 434–72.

Libet, B. (1985), 'Unconscious cerebral initiative and the role of conscious will in voluntary action', *Behavioral and Brain Sciences*, 8, 529–66.

Libet, Benjamin, Freeman, Anthony and Sutherland, Keith (eds) (1999), *The Volitional Brain: Towards a Neuroscience of Free Will*. Exeter: Imprint Academic.

Libet, Benjamin, Wright, E. W. and Gleason, C. A. (1982), 'Readiness potentials preceding unrestricted spontaneous pre-planned voluntary acts', *Electroencephalography and Clinical Neurophysiology*, 54, 322–5.

Libet, B., Wright, E. W. Jr, Feinstein, B. and Pearl, D. K. (1979), 'Subjective referral of the timing for a conscious sensory experience: a functional role for the somatosensory specific projection system in man', *Brain*, 102, 191–222.

Liljeström, Marianne and Paasonen, Susanna (eds) (2010), *Working with Affect in Feminist Readings: Disturbing Differences*. London and New York: Routledge.

Love, Heather (2010), 'Close but not deep: literary ethics and the descriptive turn', *New Literary History*, 41: 2, 371–91.

McDonald, Ronan (2018), 'Critique and anti-critique', *Textual Practice*, 32: 3, 365–74.

McGuire, Ann and Buchbinder, David (2010), 'The forensic gothic: knowledge, the supernatural, and the psychic detective', *Canadian Review of American Studies*, 40: 3, 289–307.

Marcus, George E. (1999), *Paranoia Within Reason: A Casebook on Conspiracy as Explanation*. Chicago: University of Chicago Press.

Marcus, George E. and Fischer, Michael J. (1986), *Anthropology as Cultural Critique: An Experimental Moment in the Human Sciences*. Chicago and London: University of Chicago Press.

Mariani, Philomena (1991), *Critical Fictions: The Politics of Imaginative Writing*. London: New Press.

Markel, Lester (1972), 'So what's new?', *American Editor: Bulletin of the American Society of Newspaper Editors*, January, 7–10.

Marx, Karl, and Engels, Friedrich ([1875] 1974), *Capital*. Moscow: Progress Publishers.

Massumi, Brian (1995), 'The autonomy of affect', *Cultural Critique*, 31, 83–109.

Massumi, Brian (2002), *Parables for the Virtual: Movement, Affect, Sensation*. Durham, NC and London: Duke University Press.

Mazlish, Bruce (1989), *A New Science: The Breakdown of Connections and the Birth of Sociology*. New York: Oxford University Press.

Meillassoux, Quentin (2008), *After Finitude: An Essay on the Necessity of Contingency*, trans. Ray Brassier. London and New York: Continuum.

Melley, Timothy (2000), *Empire of Conspiracy: The Culture of Paranoia in Postwar America*. Ithaca: Cornell University Press.

Menand, Louis (2005), 'Dangers within and without', *Profession*, pp. 10–17.

Merton, Robert K. (1968), *Social Theory and Social Structure*. New York: Free Press.

Miller, Carolyn (1984), 'Genre as social action', *Quarterly Journal of Speech,* 70, 151–67.

Miller, D. A. (1988), *The Novel and the Police*. Berkeley: University of California Press.

Miller, Nancy K. (2007), 'The entangled self: genre bondage in the age of the memoir', *Changing Profession*, 122: 2, 537–48.

Miller, Nancy K. (2011), *The Things They Saved: Pieces of a Jewish Past*. Lincoln: University of Nebraska Press.

Mitchell, Joseph (1992), *Up in the Old Hotel, and Other Stories*. New York: Pantheon Books.

Muecke, Stephen (2002), 'The fall: fictocritical writing', *Parallax*, 8: 4, 108–12.

Muecke, Stephen (2010), 'Public thinking, public feeling: research tools for creative writing', *TEXT*, 14: 1, online: <http://www.textjournal.com.au/april10/muecke.htm> (accessed 20 January 2017).

Naparsteck, Martin and O'Brien, Tim (1991), 'An Interview with Tim O'Brien', *Contemporary Literature*, 32: 1, 1–11.

Neilson, Brett and Rossiter, Ned (2008), 'Precarity as a political concept, or, Fordism as exception', *Theory, Culture & Society*, 25: 7–8, 51–72.

Ngai, Sianne (2005), *Ugly Feelings*. Cambridge, MA: Harvard University Press.

Nietzsche, Friedrich Wilhelm ([1888] 1968), *Twilight of the Idols; and, The Anti-Christ*, trans. R. J. Hollingdale. London: Penguin.

Nisbet, Robert A. (1966), *The Sociological Tradition*. New York: Basic Books.

Nock, A. D. (1933), *Conversion: The Old and the New in Religion from Alexander the Great to Augustine of Hippo*. Oxford: Oxford University Press.

Noys, Benjamin (2010), *The Persistence of the Negative: A Critique of Contemporary Continental Theory*. Edinburgh: Edinburgh University Press.

O'Donnell, Patrick (2000), *Latent Destinies: Cultural Paranoia and Contemporary U.S. Narrative*. Durham, NC: Duke University Press.

Oxford English Dictionaries (2016), 'Word of the year 2016 is . . . post-truth', https://languages.oup.com/word-of-the-year/word-of-the-year-2016

Otzick, Cynthia (1973), 'Reconsideration: Truman Capote', *New Republic*, 27 January, 31–4.

Papoulias, Constantina and Callard, Felicity (2010), Biology's gift: interrogating the turn to affect', *Body & Society*, 16: 1, 29–56.

Parish, Jane and Parker, Martin (eds) (2001), *The Age of Anxiety: Conspiracy Theory and the Human Sciences*. Oxford: Blackwell.

Parsons, Keith (ed.) (2003), *The Science Wars: Debating Scientific Knowledge and Technology*. Amherst, MA: Prometheus Books.

Peters, Gerald (1993), *The Mutilating God: Authorship and Authority in the Narrative of Conversion*, Amherst, MA: University of Massachusetts Press.

Pickering, Mary (1994), *Auguste Comte: An Intellectual Biography, Volume 1*. Cambridge: Cambridge University Press.

Plato and R. L. Hunter (2004), *Plato's Symposium*. New York: Oxford University Press.

Probyn, Elspeth (2005), *Blush: Faces of Shame*. Sydney: University of New South Wales Press.

Ricœur, Paul (1970), *Freud and Philosophy: An Essay on Interpretation*. New Haven: Yale University Press.

Romano, Angela (2017), 'Asserting journalistic autonomy in the "post-truth" era of "alternative facts": lessons from reporting on the orations of a populist leader', *Asia Pacific Media Educator*, 17: 1, 51–66.

Rosenfeld, Aaron S. (2004), 'The "scanty plot": Orwell, Pynchon, and the poetics of paranoia', *Twentieth Century Literature*, 50: 4, 337–67.

Said, Edward (1978), *Orientalism*. New York: Vintage Books.

Schlink, Bernhard (1997), *The Reader*. London: Phoenix House.

Schlink, Bernhard (2009), *Guilt about the Past*. St Lucia: University of Queensland Press.

Sedgwick, Eve Kosofsky (1985), *Between Men: English Literature and Male Homosocial Desire*. New York: Columbia University Press.

Sedgwick, Eve Kosofsky (1990), *Epistemology of the Closet*. Berkeley: University of California Press.

Sedgwick, Eve Kosofsky (1997), 'Paranoid reading and reparative reading; or, you're so paranoid, you probably think this introduction is about you', in *Novel Gazing: Queer Readings in Fiction*. Durham, NC and London: Duke University Press, pp. 10–39.

Sedgwick, Eve Kosofsky (2007), 'Melanie Klein and the difference affect makes', *South Atlantic Quarterly*, 106: 3, 625–43.

Sedgwick, Eve Kosofsky and Frank, Adam (1995), 'Shame in the cybernetic fold: reading Silvan Tomkins', *Critical Inquiry*, 21: 2, 496–522.

Seigel, Mark (1976), 'Creative paranoia: understanding the system of *Gravity's Rainbow*', *Critique*, 18, 39–54.

Seyfert, Robert (2012), Beyond personal feelings and collective emotions: toward a theory of social affect', *Theory, Culture & Society*, 29: 6, 27–46.

Shouse, Eric (2005), 'Feeling, emotion, affect', *M/C Journal*, 8: 6, online: <http://journal.media-culture.org.au/0512/03-shouse.php> (accessed 22 January 2017).

Snow, C. P. ([1959] 1998), *The Two Cultures*. Cambridge: Cambridge University Press.

Sokal, Alan D. (1996a), 'Transgressing the boundaries: towards a transformative hermeneutics of quantum gravity', *Social Text*, 46/47, 217–52.

Sokal, Alan D. (1996b), 'A physicist experiments with cultural studies', *Lingua Franca*, May/June, 62–4.

Solnit, Rebecca (2013), *The Faraway Nearby*. New York: Penguin.

Spinoza, Benedictus de ([1677] 2001), *Ethics*, trans. W. H. White and A. H. Stirling. London: Wordsworth Editions.

Standing, Guy (2011a), *The Precariat: The New Dangerous Class*. London: Bloomsbury.

Standing, Guy (2011b), 'Who will be a voice for the emerging precariat?', *The Guardian*, 1 June, online: http://www.guardian.co.uk/commentisfree/2011/jun/01/voice-for-emerging-precariat (accessed 16 October 2015).

Stein, Gertrude (1914), *Tender Buttons*. New York: Claire Marie.

Stengers, Isabelle (2015), *In Catastrophic Times: Resisting the Coming Barbarism*. London: Open Humanities Press.

Stewart, Kathleen (1999), 'Conspiracy theory's worlds', *Paranoia within Reason: A Casebook on Conspiracy as Explanation*, ed. George Marcus. Chicago: University of Chicago Press, pp. 13–20.

Stewart, Kathleen (2000), 'Real American dreams (can be nightmares)', *Cultural Studies and Political Theory*, ed. Jodi Dean. Ithaca: Cornell University Press, pp. 243–57.

Stewart, Kathleen (2007), *Ordinary Affects*. Durham, NC and London: Duke University Press.

Stewart, Kathleen (2008), 'Weak theory in an unfinished world', *Journal of Folklore Research*, 45: 1, 71–82.

Stewart, Kathleen (2010), 'Atmospheric attunements', *Environment and Planning D: Society and Space*, 29: 3, 445–53, online: <http://www.envplan.com/abstract.cgi?id=d9109> (accessed 18 January 2011).

Stewart, Kathleen and Harding, Susan (1999), 'Bad endings: American apocalypsis', *Annual Review of Anthropology*, 28, 285–310.

Stewart, Kathleen and Harding, Susan (2003), 'Anxieties of influence: conspiracy theory and therapeutic culture in millennial America', in Todd Saunders and Harry West (eds), *Transparency and Conspiracy: Ethnographies of Suspicion in the New World Order*. Durham, NC and London: Duke University Press, pp. 258–86.

Strathern, Marilyn (1987), 'Out of context: the persuasive fictions of anthropology', *Current Anthropology*, 28: 3, 251–81.

Strauss, David L. (2005), 'The magic of the state: an interview with Michael Taussig', *Cabinet*, 18, online: <http://www.cabinet-magazine.org/issues/18/strauss.php> (accessed 4 May 2012).

Strout, Cushing (1980), 'Historicizing fiction and fictionalizing history: the case of E. L. Doctorow', *Prospects*, 5, 423–37.

Sturken, Marita (1997), 'Reenactment, fantasy, and the paranoia of history: Oliver Stone's docudramas', *History and Theory*, 36: 4, 64–79.

Sturm, Hertha (1987), *Emotional Effects of Media: The Work of Hertha Sturm*, ed. Gertrude Joch Robinson. Montreal: McGill University.

Tamboukou, Maria (2011), 'Portraits of moments: visual and textual entanglements in narrative research', *Current Narratives*, 3, 3–13.

Tandoc, Edson, Ling, Rich, Westlund, Oscar, Duffy, Andrew M., Goh, Debbie and Wei, Lim (2018), 'Audiences' acts of authentication in the age of fake news: a conceptual framework', *New Media & Society*, 20: 8, 2745–63.

Taussig, Michael (1997), *The Magic of the State*. London and New York: Routledge.

Taussig, Michael (2010), 'The corn-wolf: writing apotropaic texts', *Critical Inquiry*, 37: 1, 26–33.

Thein, Deborah (2005), 'After or beyond feeling: a consideration of affect and emotion in Geography', *Area*, 37, 450–4.

Thomas, W. I. and Thomas, D. S. (1928), *The Child in America: Behaviour Problems and Program*. New York: Knopf.

Thrift, Nigel (2004), 'Intensities of feeling: towards a spatial politics of affect', *Geografiska Annaler*, 86: 1, 57–78.

Thrift, Nigel (2007), *Non-representational Theory: Space, Politics, Affect*. London and New York: Routledge.

Tomkins, Silvan (2008), *Affect Imagery Consciousness*. New York: Springer.

Towers, Robert (1988), 'From the grassy knoll', *New York Review of Books*, 18 August.

Trask, Michael (2010), 'Patricia Highsmith's method', *American Literary History*, 22: 3, 584–614.

Tronzo, William (ed.) (2009), *The Fragment: An Incomplete History*. Los Angeles: Getty Research Institute.

Vannini, Phillip and Williams, J. Patrick (eds) (2009), *Authenticity in Culture, Self, and Society*. Farnham and Burlington, VT: Ashgate.

Vrasti, Wanda (2011), '"Caring" capitalism and the duplicity of critique', *Theory & Event*, 14: 4, 1–17.

Warner, Michael (2004), 'Uncritical reading', *Polemic: Critical or Uncritical*, ed. Jane Gallop. New York: Routledge, pp. 13–38.

Wells, H. G. (1914), *An Englishman Looks at the World: Being a Series of Unrestrained Remarks upon Contemporary Matters*, Penn State Electronic Classics Series, online: <http://www2.hn.psu. edu/faculty/jmanis/hgwells/englishman-world.pdf> (accessed 4 February 2013).

Wetherell, Margaret (2012), *Affect and Emotion: A New Social Science Understanding*. Los Angeles and London: Sage.

Wetherell, M. (2015), 'Trends in the turn to affect: a social psychological critique', *Body & Society*, 21: 2, 139–66.

Williams, Raymond (1976), *Keywords: A Vocabulary of Culture and Society*. Oxfordshire: Croom Helm.

Wolfe, Tom (ed.) (1975), *The New Journalism*. London: Picador.

Zournazi, Mary (2002), *Hope: New Philosophies for Change*. New York: Routledge.

Index

Note: page references with 'n' indicates footnotes.

EU representative:
Easy Access System Europe
Mustamäe tee 50, 10621 Tallinn, Estonia
Gpsr.requests@easproject.com